PRENTICE-HALL
FOUNDATIONS OF MODERN SOCIOLOGY SERIES

W9-BNY-925

**PRENTICE-HALL**
**FOUNDATIONS OF MODERN SOCIOLOGY SERIES**
Alex Inkeles, Editor

INDUSTRIAL SOCIOLOGY
*Ivar Berg*

INTRODUCTION TO SOCIAL RESEARCH, Second Edition
*Ann Bonar Blalock/Hubert M. Blalock, Jr.*

RACE AND ETHNIC RELATIONS
*Hubert M. Blalock, Jr.*

DEVIANCE AND CONTROL
*Albert K. Cohen*

MODERN ORGANIZATIONS
*Amitai Etzioni*

SOCIAL PROBLEMS
*Amitai Etzioni*

LAW AND SOCIETY: An Introduction
*Lawrence M. Friedman*

THE FAMILY
*William J. Goode*

SOCIETY AND POPULATION, Second Edition
*David M. Heer*

WHAT IS SOCIOLOGY? An Introduction to the Discipline and Profession
*Alex Inkeles*

THE SOCIOLOGY OF SMALL GROUPS
*Theodore M. Mills*

SOCIAL CHANGE, Second Edition
*Wilbert E. Moore*

THE SOCIOLOGY OF RELIGION
*Thomas F. O'Dea*

THE EVOLUTION OF SOCIETIES
*Talcott Parsons*

RURAL SOCIETY
*Irwin T. Sanders*

THE AMERICAN SCHOOL: A Sociological Analysis
*Patricia C. Sexton*

THE SOCIOLOGY OF ECONOMIC LIFE, Second Edition
*Neil J. Smelser*

FOUNDATIONS OF MODERN SOCIOLOGY
*Metta Spencer/Alex Inkeles*

SOCIAL STRATIFICATION: The Forms and Functions of Inequality
*Melvin M. Tumin*

# INTRODUCTION
# TO SOCIAL RESEARCH

second edition

# INTRODUCTION TO SOCIAL RESEARCH

ANN BONAR BLALOCK
*Social Policy Consultant*

HUBERT M. BLALOCK, JR.
*University of Washington*

Prentice-Hall, Inc., Englewood Cliffs, New Jersey 07632

*Library of Congress Cataloging in Publication Data*

BLALOCK, ANN B.
   Introduction to social research.

   Rev. ed. of: An introduction to social
research / Hubert M. Blalock, Jr. 1st ed. 1970.
      Bibliography: p.
      Includes index.
      1. Social sciences—Research.  I. Blalock,
Hubert M.  II. Blalock, Hubert M.  Introduction
to social research.  III. Title.
H62.B575      1982      300′.72        81–15876
ISBN   0–13–496810–7                   AACR2
ISBN   0–13–496802–6 (pbk.)

Editorial/production supervision and interior design by A. Roney
Manufacturing buyer: John B. Hall

Printed in the United States of America

10  9  8  7  6  5  4  3  2  1

ISBN 0-13-496802-6 {P}
ISBN 0-13-496810-7 {C}

Prentice-Hall International, Inc., *London*
Prentice-Hall of Australia Pty. Limited, *Sydney*
Prentice-Hall of Canada, Ltd., *Toronto*
Prentice-Hall of India Private Limited, *New Delhi*
Prentice-Hall of Japan, Inc., *Tokyo*
Prentice-Hall of Southeast Asia Pte. Ltd., *Singapore*
Whitehall Books Limited, *Wellington, New Zealand*

To Rosemary Sharp, an anthropologist, psychologist, and close friend of many years, whose creative teaching has consistently interested students of social science in the complex relationships between individuals and societies, and the necessity of directing competent social research to their exploration.

In memory of David Varley, one of the finest teachers of sociology we have known, with whom we shared a long and very valuable friendship.

# CONTENTS

CHAPTER 7

# PREFACE

The purpose of this book is to interest you in some of the basic issues of research in the social sciences. The quantitative aspects of this research have become increasingly technical, resulting in increased communication difficulties between the social researcher and the consumer of research, and within the social science community itself. Social scientists have therefore needed to make special efforts to describe the research process in clear and simple terms, and to provide those who are interested in increasing their research knowledge with a realistic perspective on the limitations and problems of research, and on its accomplishments and possibilities. An expected benefit of exploring these issues is a greater appreciation of the complexities involved in integrating our theories with our facts.

In this effort we have appreciated the ideas and insights of colleagues with whom we have discussed research, and particularly the very important and useful comments of the formal reviewers. We feel a very special gratitude to Sandy Brown. Her technical expertise in recommending styles and formats and in preparing the manuscript for the publisher, her sensitivity to organization and expression, and her patience and support were invaluable.

Our children have also made a significant contribution, having been remarkably alert to the research potential in marital co-authorship and its inherent problems and possibilities. They have provided encouragement and avoided controversy at almost all the right times, in the context of an appropriately inquiring curiosity.

Ann Bonar Blalock/Hubert M. Blalock, Jr.

# INTRODUCTION
# TO SOCIAL RESEARCH

# CHAPTER 1
# THE CONTEXT OF SOCIAL RESEARCH

Our minds are finite, and yet even in these circumstances of finitude we are surrounded by possibilities that are infinite, and the purpose of human life is to grasp as much as we can out of that infinitude.*

Most social scientists take as their world to study those complex, intricate social phenomena that describe the environments in which individuals and social institutions interact. Some of these phenomena, defined by the society's decision makers as "social problems," have historically been of particular interest to the social science researcher. Paradoxically, although social scientists are well qualified to investigate the content and context of these problems, they have had only minimal influence in defining them and developing alternatives for solving them. These responsibilities have been assigned to others, largely through social, economic, and political processes, rather than academic or scientific ones.

Ultimately, most policy decisions are made outside the scientific community. The primary motivation underlying these processes shaping policy has often been to "maintain the system," to preserve or restore a level of organization and functioning considered satisfactory by those in positions of authority, responsibility, and power. Social problems must often reach threshold levels, beyond which acquiescence is considered less preferable than action, before commissions, task forces, or new government divisions are created, studies begun, and short-term policy recommendations made. Therefore, decisions have frequently been made in response to events per-

* The quotations used at the beginning of each chapter are from Alfred North Whitehead.

ceived as social, economic, or political crises, rather than on the basis of ongoing systematic investigation of underlying causes and effects, the anticipation and prevention of problems, or the identification of possibilities for positive change.

A good example is President Johnson's appointment of a commission to conduct a time-limited study of the causes of the disastrous riots of the summer of 1967 generated by racial unrest. Major policy decisions were to be based on this short-term study. In the aftermath of the Martin Luther King and Robert Kennedy assassinations, he appointed a second blue-ribbon commission to study the causes of assassinations. Both groups were composed of a large number of elected officials representing both parties, plus a few black leaders, clergymen, and labor union representatives. Interestingly enough, no social scientists were appointed, in spite of the fact that for at least two decades social scientists specializing in race relations had anticipated such problems and attempted to persuade private foundations and the federal government to undertake large-scale research on minority group relations.[1] The research subject was controversial, and priorities governing the allocation of money did not support forms of research appropriate to the complexity of the problem, such as substantial pilot projects and long-term experimental studies.

Meanwhile, it was clear to social scientists that these commissions could not hope to carry out valid studies of problems this complicated. They could certainly suggest some causes and recommend some solutions, but they would likely have great difficulty applying research principles—knowing what variables to look for, controlling for these variables, and deciding how to measure their effects—while under public pressure to produce a report before the next social crisis or the next election.

Such has been the history of population problems as well, despite the long-term efforts of demographers to alert those in policy-making positions to the problem of worldwide overpopulation and its potential consequences. The same is certainly true for energy problems. The birth control issue, and the attitudes of corporations controlling major sources of energy, have, respectively, limited the investigation of these problems. Yet both issues are extremely complex and warrant large-scale research efforts over time. While competent theory and research have been appreciated in developing policy in these areas, the avoidance of confrontation and the need for immediate, acceptable answers have diminished the value of skillful research as a basis for policy decisions.

This aspect of the policy process has remained largely unchanged. What *has* changed is the role of the federal government. It has progressively become

---

1.  To the credit of the appointed commission members and their staff, however, an extensive effort was made to solicit opinions from reputable social scientists as well as other citizens. The major point is that it is impossible to conduct a scientific study, involving the actual collection and analysis of data, under such pressures.

the major funder of basic and applied research in both the physical and social sciences. This has had several significant effects, particularly on social research.

One effect is that research funding has become more dependent on public attitudes, particularly attitudes toward the economy and its ability to sustain certain kinds of spending. These attitudes are reflected in the Congress, perhaps the most powerful influence with respect to research funding. The Congress has become increasingly subject to special interest pressures, which have had a significant impact on the purpose of research and the extent of its fiscal support. The federal courts play an important indirect role through decisions that mandate research or that result in future legislation affecting research activities. The Executive Branch sets decisive precedents for what issues deserve research attention, and defines the limits within which federal agencies develop research objectives and budgets for Congressional action. Annual governmental budget cycles, and changing policy makers and administrators, further limit long-term research studies.

The expansion of governmental responsibilities has created an additional effect in the form of a growing public demand for greater funding *accountability*—that is, proof of the benefits resulting from tax monies spent. This has required government to produce better evidence of whether tax-supported policy initiatives and social programs are achieving goals considered appropriate by elected officials and special interest groups. To provide the evidence requested, research has become a required component of many statutes and regulations authorizing social programs and projects.

Government support of research, however, has gradually shifted in emphasis from grants for studies seeking information on generic social science issues such as poverty, racism, social movements, large-scale organizations, or deviant behavior, to contracts for shorter-term research projects such as the evaluation of the effectiveness of specific social programs. This trend reflects the increasing strength of utilitarian values and pragmatic preferences compatible with the interests of those constituencies that legitimize government authority.

Consequently, there has been a rapid development of policy-oriented research in response to the increase in government contracts designed to satisfy a particular kind of accountability—i.e., accountability sometimes defined mainly in terms of strictly monetary costs measured against somewhat narrow perceptions of social benefits. Proposals for these contracts are often reviewed by administrators rather than researchers, and a large number of the major government contracts for policy-related social research are awarded to independent research firms rather than to the academic community. Social scientists, with the exception of applied economists, are frequently underrepresented on the staffs of such firms.

The flourishing of policy research has not involved substantially larger numbers of social scientists in policy-making positions, nor has it become a primary career for very many social researchers. It led initially to an influx of professionals with minimal research training and has often resulted in poor research. At the same time, however, it has provided a new opportunity for well-trained social researchers to study issues of great interest to them, research questions to which they can make an important contribution.

An increased movement of competent scientists into contract research has raised research standards substantially in a number of policy areas. Their research findings have enriched the general knowledge base and improved the formulation of policy alternatives. Also, increasing government responsibility and stronger accountability pressures have created a new public awareness of the value of research, and have given it greater public credibility and prestige. However, with tighter controls being exercised over the conduct of contract research, government regulation of social research has been more pervasive. Such regulation has made it difficult to test a range of theory and apply research designs and methods appropriate to the complexity of the social issues being studied.

The social and political environment of social research, with its intriguing collection of public interests, anxieties, and political priorities, strongly affects the nature of social research in important, continuing ways: the research problems selected, the goals of the research, its assumptions, the subjects to be studied, the inferences to be drawn from findings, and its use. Large-scale research efforts intended to give attention to *prediction* and *prevention* hold less attraction than short-term projects whose purpose is remedial and ameliorative. Research emphasizing the investigation of the complex *causes* of social phenomena is given less support than research describing the effects. The latter often assume immediate importance because of the pressures applied by powerful constituencies.

While understandable organizationally, this sometimes has the unanticipated consequence of denying the society full use of social science expertise in achieving the broader goals of producing, communicating, and utilizing valid knowledge explaining social phenomena. It may deprive the society of the critical inferences and insights that could have been obtained from more rigorous research. If so, this would limit the application of scientific insights in identifying and resolving social problems, and experimenting with new options for improving life quality.

The comparative powerlessness of social scientists to affect the outcomes of social policy has generated a great deal of interesting debate. Some scientists argue that the goals and strategies of science should be kept separate from those of policy. Others insist that social science and social policy are inevitably intertwined. The controversy raises the basic question of what purpose social research should serve. A consensus exists that one of its primary functions is to increase the knowledge base that explains relationships between the major forces in society. There is general agreement that the enrichment of such a knowledge base, through the continued development and refinement of theory and research, provides the best basis for the formulation of rational, enlightened social policy. But social scientists have not been particularly adept in communicating these ideas to others.

Therefore social scientists must assume some of the responsibility for the predicament in which they find themselves. They may not have made a strong enough effort to clarify, pragmatically, the value of the research process and precisely what it involves. Scientific journals have often overused jargon, while popular writing on social science issues has frequently failed to explain adequately how and why research is done. The public has been left with an unclear or naïve impression of the research process and its implications.

Social researchers have been less than willing and eager to challenge the idea that cold, hard statistics and concrete, empirical data are not as crucial to the development of knowledge as intuitive insights and observations. They have not emphasized sufficiently the necessity of viewing social phenomena as complex problems to which equally complex methods must be applied. In response to the needs and demands of policy analysts, politicians, and agency administrators for immediate answers to specific questions, social scientists have often hesitated to suggest that good answers involve a calculated price that includes the sponsorship of long-range basic research as well as shorter-term applied research. They have not always admitted honestly that for some questions only partial answers can be obtained, or sometimes literally no answers, given our present limited knowledge. They have sometimes refused to work with the public, the government, or the private sector to increase their understanding and acceptance of the answers that *are* produced. In general, social scientists have not always been the most effective advocates for what they believe and do.

Those oriented to action in the policy arena are often subjected to realistic pressures to develop quick practical solutions rather than to carry on research designed to study the basic issues. Better income maintenance programs, increased public housing, more jobs, or more adequate education take precedence over research the public tends to view as a simple documentation of *why* these are needed. In this context, the intricate cause-and-effect aspects of these issues seem less important than the need for immediate solutions. The important relationships between economic and social influences and the level of social welfare provision, the guaranteeing of full employment, or the restructuring of education are often not perceived as high priority. Research, in fact, is sometimes mistakenly identified as an expensive exercise in confirming common sense. As a result, the benefits of a more sophisticated research perspective in developing and evaluating alternative policies and programs is frequently lost. And the significance of basic research, which permits the accumulation of usable knowledge on which future options can more rationally be based, may unfortunately be neglected.

# THE COMPLEXITY OF SOCIAL RESEARCH

One of the basic difficulties encountered in social research that needs to be communicated more effectively is the existence of a large number of variables that are highly interrelated. In many cases, their causes and effects are hard to disentangle, and there may be almost as many theories or explanations as there are people to formulate them. Policy development, planning, and social research become exceedingly difficult in this situation, and individual biases and ideological differences may predominate. It is simple to fall back on the disclaimer that objective social science is impossible and that such questions must ultimately be resolved by what are essentially political means. The social scientist's answer to this thesis must be resolute.

There must be agreement that the task is a complicated and sometimes frustrating one, and that we should not expect anywhere near the degree of precision that is found in the physical sciences. But this does not mean that steady improvement cannot be made in our theories, methods of data collection and analysis, and in the quality of the data. We must, however, clearly distinguish between the kinds of questions that can and cannot be answered by scientific means. While questions of what *should* be the state of affairs, what is right and wrong, who deserves what, and so forth, are questions that cannot be answered by scientific procedures, there are many questions that can be resolved by these means. In particular, the scientist can make conditional statements of the form "if such and such a state of affairs is desired, then the following means appear to be most efficient," or "if $A$ then $B$." This kind of information is surely valuable for the policy maker, though admittedly at present we can make very few simple assertions with any degree of confidence. More realistically, the aim is to provide propositions of the form "Under conditions $A$, $B$, and $C$, if $X$ were increased, then $Y$ and $Z$ can be expected to increase."

To illustrate the kind of complexity with which social scientists must deal, consider ethnic prejudice and discrimination. A substantial amount of social research has been devoted in the past to documenting different forms of prejudice and the extent of discrimination, and to measuring different degrees of these two phenomena. For example, research findings indicate that Jews are generally less prejudiced toward racial minorities than are Protestants and Catholics, that residential segregation of blacks varies very little from city to city, that the population of blacks has increased in the central cities, that residential segregation is only weakly related to the percentage of blacks in an area or to their income levels, and that industrial unions are less discriminatory than craft unions. Many of these facts are now well known to the general public, though some are not obvious or easily explained by common sense.

The so-called cycle of poverty, as it affects the minority population, has been well documented and publicized. We know that a disproportionate number of minorities tend to have low incomes, inadequate education, insufficient jobs, high unemployment rates, high disease rates, and high "alienation" scores, all of which *predispose* individuals to poverty. And these factors appear to be causally interrelated. Most would agree that this general statement about poverty is largely accurate as far as it goes. But whenever one finds a large number of factors that are related in this way, one is tempted to select a few preferred choices as the basic causes. However, this allows a wide degree of discretion and ample opportunities for ideological biases to operate.

Imagine, for example, how a proverbial white conservative or liberal might explain the cycle of poverty, ignoring the more naïve one-factor explanations such as "the innate inferiority of minorities" or "the inherent defects of capitalism." The stereotypical conservative may accept the fact that whites tend to be prejudiced and that minorities have faced discrimination, but may place the burden of responsibility for change on minorities themselves. The conservative may insist that prejudice cannot be eliminated simply by passing laws, that minorities must prove themselves deserving and learn to assimilate through their own efforts. He or she may claim that a great outlay of public funds for the unemployed and poor is inappropriate. In contrast, the stereotypical liberal may view prejudiced attitudes and discriminatory behavior as the fundamental reasons for the economic, educational, and occupational difficulties of minorities. The liberal may insist that we cannot break the cycle of poverty unless minorities are compensated for inequities in education, employment, housing, and income that result from institutional racism.

Elaborations on these two interpretations, and their many variants, essentially assign causal importance to very different factors. The first perspective stresses the minority person's responsibility to improve his or her situation by taking advantage of the opportunities available, independent of the social context. The second assumes that the minority person's behavior is almost entirely conditioned by the social environment—i.e., by the behavior of the white majority. There is, of course, some truth in both assessments. However, neither identifies the causes and effects of poverty through a systematic study of a remarkably complex set of interrelated problems.

The major challenge confronting the social scientist is that of deciding objectively which influences should receive the greatest weight in explaining particular phenomena. The key question is how to use the principles of scientific method, broadly interpreted, to judge the relative importance of diverse social forces—rather than relying on compelling rhetoric, political persuasion, or personal philosophy. If the approach taken lacks objectivity and thoroughness, our ultimate assessments will be determined by our own value biases and self-interests.

Certain problems make it difficult to provide really definitive answers to many important questions that might be asked of the social scientist. Some of these difficulties are shared by all the sciences and stem from limitations inherent in the scientific method. Some are purely technical and have not yet been satisfactorily resolved. Others can be resolved but the data are currently lacking, either because no one had thought of studying the question, or because researchers were prevented from investigating it.

For those wishing to study society, fully recognizing that solutions to research questions and social problems will rarely be simple or immediate, this brief introduction to research indicates the magnitude of the task. The emphasis in the remaining chapters is on the many complexities encountered in the research process. In discussing these, it is often much easier to focus on the complications than to overcome them, since the latter requires considerably more technical knowledge and resources. However, those who underestimate or ignore these difficulties will pay a price later. Undertaking serious research in the social sciences, or acquiring a knowledge of its dimensions as competent research consumers and users, demands that both the possibilities and the problems be approached openly and honestly.

## THE RESEARCH PROCESS

The purpose of research is to apply the scientific method to the complex task of discovering answers to questions. The scientific method is a set of procedures and guidelines designed to increase the probability that the information gathered in investigating questions will yield relevant, reliable, unbiased, and valid answers. No research ever quite reaches that impressive goal, but the scientific research process is more likely to do so than other means.

The scientific method can be summarized simply as follows:

—the statement of the research problem or issue to be investigated, or the *theoretical explanation* to be tested;
—the translation of the abstract ideas in this theoretical explanation into concrete, explicitly identifiable ideas;
—the development of *measures* of the important variables in the theoretical explanation;
—the development of a research *design* to guide the inquiry into the research problem, so that the information gathered truly tests the validity of the explanation to the fullest extent possible;
—the selection of a set of *methods* that implement this design;
—the collection of the research data;
—the *analysis* of this information in the context of the proposed explanation; and
—the *interpretation* of the information, or integration of the findings of the research with the existing knowledge base.

Though in practice this series of integrated activities is never pursued in perfect chronological order by the researcher, the logic of this sequence is difficult to question. Design, measurement, data collection techniques, and analytic strategies may be brilliantly conceived and implemented; but if there is no meaningful framework for bringing together the results of the research so that the new information supports, expands, revises, or rejects previous explanations, the research has not advanced us terribly far. On the other hand, the theoretical explanation may be clearly and precisely formulated, and the researcher eminently equipped to implement an appropriate research design, but the definitions of the major variables, and the way they are measured to produce research data, may not adequately reflect the true qualities of the phenomenon being studied. Or the theoretical explanation may again be excellently thought out and data collection techniques well in hand, but the research design does not adequately control for the effect of competing explanations, leaving in doubt the value of the data collected and complicating the analysis. Or finally, perhaps the analysis and interpretation of the data may be extremely sophisticated and thorough, but the data unreliably collected and therefore of little validity.

In this sense, the steps in the research process, based on the logical steps of the scientific method, represent a series of prerequisites, the achievement of which predisposes the research process to a more or less successful conclusion. No precise evaluation can ever be made of the relative importance of "each step to the whole" for any one research project. And even the best research contains deficiencies at one point or another in that process. Nevertheless, in general, the more adequate the resolution of each set of tasks in the logical sequence, the more useful the research in producing new knowledge and suggesting fresh explanations for future study. This point of view expresses the organizing philosophy of this introduction to social research.

# CHAPTER 2
# THEORY

All the world over and at all times there have been practical men, absorbed in irreducible and stubborn facts; all the world over and at all times there have been men of philosophic temperament, who have been absorbed in the weaving of general principles.

You may feel some confusion and surprise that we are beginning a book on research with a discussion of theory. It is true that theory and research are often thought of as separate entities. However, our intention is to dispel such a belief. In reality, theory and research represent two interrelated activities, both of which are integral to the research process. Individual social scientists may vary in their interests, preferences, and skills in performing theoretical tasks as compared to research tasks, but both tasks are essential to social research.

The temptation to dichotomize theoretical and empirical efforts should be resisted, as they represent a continuum of highly interdependent activities. The researcher must integrate these activities in achieving the ultimate goal of research: the enhancement of knowledge. Useless distinctions between theory and research may limit the repertoire of skills a researcher applies to the problem selected, excluding a very stimulating area of work that provides unique opportunities for creativity and innovation. The excitement of seeking answers to questions is rivaled only by the exhilaration of selecting and developing the questions for which answers can be sought.

Let us reconsider some common-sense notions of the differences between theory and research. The term "theoretical" sometimes connotes something very general, abstract, highly speculative, and at best tentative: It is primarily a product of reasoning. Research is often viewed as something very specific, concrete, pragmatic, and tangible: It is more a product of action. The scientific meaning of theory, however, unquestionably places it at the beginning of the research process, consistent with the tenets of the scientific method.

A *theory* is essentially an explanation of the relationships and underlying principles that appear to characterize the particular phenomenon the researcher selects to study. Such an explanation consists of a set of statements that describe close associations or causal relationships between certain influential factors, or *variables*. Theoretical *propositions* are simple statements that can be investigated by using a number of research approaches. *Hypotheses* are more specific statements of relationships that are phrased such that these relationships can be tested—i.e., systematically studied with the intention of supporting or rejecting them. For example, if we wanted to study some aspect of the phenomenon "youth crime," we might investigate the relationship between the variable "degree of trust in the youth's relationship with his or her parents," or the variable "level of peer group approval for the youth's criminal deviance," and the variable "number of reported crimes against property committed by the youth." We would begin with an explanation that described how these variables might be related. One proposition might be that adolescent peer attitudes that reward criminal behavior are one cause of youth crime. Another might be that parent-child relationships involving a high degree of trust will discourage criminal behavior. A research hypothesis would require prior commitment to a method for measuring the variables in such proposed relationships, in a very specific context. For instance, one hypothesis might be that there will be a negative relationship between trust and reported crime, the measures for the variables "trust" and "reported crime" having been designated explicitly. In stating such relationships, we would be taking certain things for granted, such as how social learning and its reinforcement take place.

Ideally, research is based on testing a manageable set of hypotheses, or exploring a limited number of theoretical propositions. The statements, in either case, represent qualities or properties that the researcher assumes explain the phenomenon under investigation. This explanation of relationships, or *theoretical model*, specifies the nature of the relationships between those variables thought to be contributing most significantly to the phenomenon studied. The variables thought responsible for producing the effects described are commonly referred to as the *independent variables*. In the example, the parent-child relationship and peer group attitudes are independent variables. They are viewed as producing the effect. Those considered the major receivers of effects are called the *dependent variables*. Criminal behavior, for instance, is the dependent variable. It is perceived as the outcome of the influence of the other variables.

Any particular variable could, therefore, conceivably serve as an independent variable in one model and a dependent one in another, based on the particular set of relationships proposed. If we wanted to study the proposition that population growth is strongly influenced by norms about family size, these norms would represent our independent variable and population growth the dependent. However, if we believed that norms about family size are affected by population growth, our independent and dependent variables would be reversed. Sometimes we must allow for the possibility of *reciprocal causation*, in which the key variables have an important effect on one another.

The forms of the relationships described in the explanatory model are not the only critical part of theory. Each model is guided by its own cluster of assumptions, premises, and possible biases, whether these are openly identified, simply implied, or must be agonizingly extracted by force from the explanation. These reveal, whether intended or not, the extent to which the research is directed by (1) the prior knowledge base (both empirical findings from previous research and the body of existing theory), (2) the degree of validity of that knowledge base, and (3) the level of integration between theoretical and empirical ideas within the knowledge base.

Some of these assumptions derive from already-tested theory. Some cannot be tested simply because the available data are not adequate. Some are inherently untestable. Irrespective of their status, the development of a science consists in substituting increasingly more realistic and useful assumptions for those less valid, so that the resulting theoretical explanation accounts for an increasing variety of facts and yields progressively more precise predictions that can be tested with research data.

We can briefly illustrate the ideas discussed so far with another simple example. Suppose we want to explain some aspect of the phenomenon "child abuse." We may have been motivated, among other things, by a pure desire for knowledge, a more specific desire to increase other scientists' awareness and understanding, or a more pragmatic desire to produce change. Putting aside for a moment the question of any prior biases in the selection of the issue, let us propose that a significant number of adult child abusers were themselves abused children, and that the abuse of children by adults is largely due to the effect of parental role modeling. There may be important rival or complementary explanations, but this is the one we have chosen. We may feel that the existing knowledge base suggests such a relationship is reasonable, or our own experience with the issue may confirm it. Our choice may reflect the vagaries of our own fantasy life about the issue, or at the very worst it may be based on the political or fiscal feasibility of explaining the phenomenon in this way. For whatever reason, we exclude other explanations from the statement of relationships, even though we may consider other factors when we carry out the actual research.

The major independent variable in this model is parental role modeling, and the dependent variable is child abuse. A very simple set of statements might be: (1) the child-abuse role played by parents causes the child to incorporate this particular behavior in his or her set of behaviors, and (2) the presence of this behavior within the individual's repertoire causes the person to abuse his or her own child as an adult. Or if hypothesis testing of causal relationships were inappropriate and a more exploratory approach indicated, the proposition might simply be that these two variables are *related*.

In applying this uncomplicated theoretical argument, certain assumptions must be made explicit. Let us suppose that the main ones are that child abusing is a learned behavior, and that parents are the major source of conditioning. More basic, let us propose that the value premise motivating the study is that child abuse is unacceptable behavior and ought to be prevented or treated. These assumptions and value judgments subtly guide the development of the theoretical explanation and, indirectly, the research process. As a result, other independent variables, such as self-esteem and frustration tolerance, interpersonal family stress, financial or occupational pressures, or perhaps alcohol or drug abuse, are excluded from the argument. While the research process can compensate for a simplistic argument to some extent, the level of sophistication of the explanation sets important limits, and sometimes substantial constraints, to the subsequent investigation of its truthfulness.

This example should alert us to an important point. The way in which scientists state the *research question*—that is, the principles, relationships, and assumptions that describe a phenomenon—affects the extent to which the full reality of what they want to study is eventually understood. Therefore it shapes the way knowledge is accumulated and integrated and affects how widely this knowledge can be generalized.

A great deal of social research is based on careful, often brilliant research plans and strategies. We can often have great confidence in the validity of its findings. It frequently suggests fresh insights and new questions for further research. The ultimate value of research, however, is greatly influenced by the theoretical approach that directs research activities, and the underlying perspective rationalizing that approach and conditioning the selection of research strategies. The adequacy of the theoretical model therefore determines the extent to which research will integrate abstract theory with factual knowledge. This is a necessity if the major goal of scientific method is to be achieved: the gradual development of general *laws* that explain patterns of relationships common to a number of phenomena and that have predictive value.

## CAUSE-AND-EFFECT RELATIONSHIPS

A social researcher may find that the data indicate that a number of variables are correlated or associated with the variable to be explained. The leap from this factual result to the conclusion that these variables are *causes* of the phenomenon in question cannot be made without the assistance of additional assumptions. This is because there will be many more correlates of a phenomenon than there are causes. The task is to reduce the number of explanatory variables by eliminating those that are related to the variable by chance or through the common influence of another variable.

The process of making causal inferences is a difficult and technical task, but essential to the fruitful interaction between theory and research. The greatest temptation is to select certain of the variables that are correlated with the variables of interest as the "true causes," and then to generate as many reasons as possible in defense of one's position. Unfortunately, persons with different biases or vested interests are equally capable of producing arguments convincing to persons of their own persuasion. Social scientists have been particularly guilty of this, though many seriously search for more objective procedures less open to the influence of personal biases.

The dispute over the role of food additives in the genesis of cancer illustrates this widespread problem and its importance. The problem has its source in a fundamental limitation of the scientific method, as well as a number of rather serious obstacles that are especially characteristic of much nonexperimental research. The difficulty is not insurmountable, though it seems to be a fact of scientific life that every time an objectionable assumption is arbitrarily eliminated (such as genetic factors in the case of cancer), a certain price has to be paid; one has to either substitute a more plausible assumption or expand the research.

In the case of experimental research, certain designs and methods resolve some but not all of these difficulties. Some of these will be discussed in Chapter 4, Research Design. In natural settings, however, variables tend to operate in an interrelated way, and it is more difficult to disentangle causes from effects. For example, the nature of family relationships affects the mental health of family members, but individual members' mental health also affects the nature of those relationships. Which factor can be sorted out as the cause and which as the effect? Or are they truly reciprocal in their cause-and-effect implications? Also, phenomena sometimes change according to a definite temporal sequence, in which case we may infer that the change that took place later did not cause the prior change. In many instances, changes in all the variables of interest take place more or less continuously, or so rapidly that they cannot be observed. In all these situations the task of sorting out cause and effect is very difficult, and the researcher may have to treat one or more untestable assumptions *as if* they were observed facts.

In the next section, we shall consider some complications that may arise in research that cannot conform to the simplicity of experimental conditions. To preface that discussion with a familiar example, let us again use the cycle of poverty, particularly in the case of minorities. In any relatively complex real-life situation, there will be numerous variables operating, requiring the researcher to deal with different kinds or classes of factors more or less simultaneously. Our first step is to construct a *model*, or a simplified version of reality in which we explicitly identify and interrelate what we assume to be the most important variables operating in a given setting. Suppose we have been able to identify six very general kinds of variables that we think are related, as indicated in Figure 2-1. In this particular model the assumption made is that factors associated with a person's family, and affecting his or her basic personality, are those in Block I. These factors are presumed to influence an individual's specific prejudices (Block II), which in turn affect the person's actual behavior toward members of the minority group (Block IV). This line of reasoning is a more or less orthodox social-psychological explanation of discrimination. But there may also be numerous situational factors (Block III) that also influence discrimination and that are causally linked to family background factors in Block I. Economists would probably focus on one cluster of Block III variables. Sociologists are more prone to emphasize a

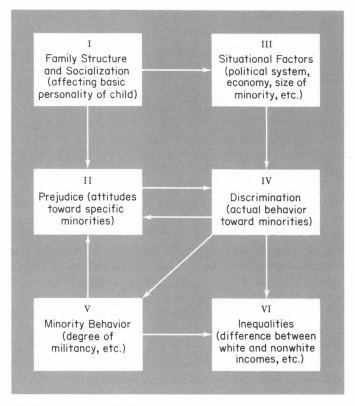

**Figure 2-1** Causal Model Postulating Relationships among Blocks of Variables

range of Block III variables than they are prejudice and family socialization. Political scientists would likely emphasize behavior (Block IV).

But the actual behavior of members of the minority group (Block V) may affect both prejudice (Block II) and any inequalities that may exist between the minority and dominant group (Block VI). The "conservative" explanation in Chapter 1 assumes causal connections that emphasize the influence of Block V on Blocks II and VI, whereas that of the "liberal" stresses the effects of Block IV on Blocks V and VI. It is possible to form a synthesis by arguing that all these factors are important, but this does not mean they are *equally* important. How can we assess the relative importance of each block of variables?

There are systematic ways of proceeding so that numerical weights can be attached to each set of factors, but all such methods require careful conceptualization of the variables in each block. They also require the accurate measurement of each variable. For example, if the variables in Block I are measured much more carefully than those in Block III, it would not be surprising to "discover" that family background factors turned out to be more important than the situational factors of Block III. Any study that is designed to evaluate the relative contributions of different sets of factors must be inclusive and thorough. Small-scale exploratory studies usually cannot be accumulated and summarized to achieve this effect.

What are the implications of the ideas just illustrated? If we knew which sets of factors were most important in affecting discrimination, or the behavior of a minority, this knowledge would be extremely useful not only for generalizing to other research problems but as a basis for intelligent policy. Of course, some variables may be more easily manipulated than others. The researcher can more readily change the values of certain kinds of variables. Also, some variables in Figure 2-1 may have direct effects on the status of the minority while others may have equally significant indirect effects.

If a theory were well established, careful measures used, and valid quantitative data collected, the researcher would be in an advantageous position to begin to answer applied questions such as, "How much would the median incomes of blacks be changed if the overall unemployment rate were reduced by 1 percent?" "If the government were to invest an additional billion dollars in improved housing, how much change in the aspirations of black youth might we expect?" "If we were to invest the same amount in improving the school system in a particular way, how much change would occur?" Obviously we are not at present able to answer such questions with the degree of precision we would like, but these questions are at least potentially answerable with a good theory and good data.

Several theoretical models involving a small number of variables are discussed in the following section to illustrate basic empirical issues that arise in the development and testing of theory. It is sufficient at this point to make one very general comment. We must always think on two levels simultaneously and then gradually bring the two together. On the first level, we try to explain a complex reality as completely as possible, considering many more variables than we can possibly measure in a single piece of research. Such a theoretical explanation may involve as many as thirty or forty variables. At the same time, we develop simplified models, containing many fewer variables, that stand a much more reasonable chance of actually being measured in a particular study. Such a model might begin with only four or five major variables, with others being added a few at a time.

As a study proceeds, some of these may prove to be totally unrelated to the dependent variable, and may then be replaced by others. In a series of subsequent studies, additional variables may be measured and included in the model, so that through a cumulative process we can begin to approximate fairly accurately the degree of complexity needed to explain the phenomenon in question. The simplified models that are tested on the second level begin, then, to approximate in complexity and sophistication the more complete theories that have been stated on the first level. Actual empirical research may show, however, that many of the variables originally thought to be important have only minimal explanatory power, in which case the degree of complexity envisaged in the more complete theory can be simplified on the basis of these research findings.

## INFERRING CAUSAL RELATIONSHIPS FROM CORRELATIONS

One of the most challenging areas of theory and research is identifying the nature and strength of the influence that one key variable has on another, particularly in terms of cause and effect. This relates to the notion of *correlation*, or the degree of association between variables. When a theoretical model proposes, for example, that perceptions of life quality are not consistently correlated with tangible indicators such as adequacy of food, housing, employment, and level of material goods, the investigator's intent is to explore whether the value of one life-quality variable is closely associated with the value of the other, or whether the *degree of association* between the two is weak or nonexistent.

In the field of statistics, the idea of degree of association is made more precise by developing concrete measures of correlation or association. These measures are constructed to have an upper limit of 1.0 whenever there is a perfect relationship between two variables that are positively related, or a lower limit of $-1.0$ whenever they are negatively, or inversely, related. These *correlation coefficients* take on the value of zero whenever there is absolutely no association between two variables, meaning that the researcher cannot predict one variable from the other any better than on the basis of chance. Correlation coefficients may also take on intermediate values, such as .3 or .5, which represent relationships where one cannot completely predict the values of one variable from the values of the other.[1,1]

To illustrate correlations further, let us assume that two variables, $X$ and $Y$, have been found to be correlated with one another, and that we want to propose in addition that $X$ is a *cause* of $Y$. Suppose that evidence exists that permits us to rule out the possibility that $Y$ causes $X$. Assume also that educational level, $X$, measured simply by two categories of years of formal schooling, is correlated with occupational choice, $Y$, measured very crudely by white-collar professional, technical, and managerial occupations versus blue-collar crafts and trades. Take for granted as well that we can rule out the possibility that occupational choice determines (causes) educational level. The following might be the results obtained in the research carried out:

Table   2-1    Hypothetical Data Showing a Relationship between Education and Occupation Choice

| Y: OCCUPATIONAL CHOICE | X: EDUCATION Less than high school degree | High school degree and beyond | TOTAL |
|---|---|---|---|
| Blue-collar | 62 | 38 | 100 |
| White-collar | 38 | 62 | 100 |
| | 100 | 100 | 200 |

The figures in the body of Table 2-1 represent 200 cases, simply for convenience. These figures show a relationship between education and occupation: persons with less than a high school degree tend to become blue-collar workers, while those with greater education tend to be white-collar workers. If the researcher wanted to gather evidence that an individual's occupational choice is at least in part due to years of formal education, he or she would need to be concerned about making the assumption that such a statement was true only if "other things were considered equal." This anxiety would be based on the fact that individuals were not randomly assigned to two groups by educational level, or kept under rigid laboratory conditions that controlled for other explanations of occupational choice. Under such conditions, the assumption that other things indeed *are* equal is much less plausible than in research carried out under experimental conditions.

For instance, suppose a person's socioeconomic background in part

---

1.  The most commonly used measure of correlation, the so-called Pearsonian correlation coefficient $r$, has the interpretation that the value of $r$, when squared, represents that proportion of the variance in one variable that is linearly associated with the other. Therefore if $r = .5$, 25 percent of the variance in $Y$ is associated with $X$, whereas an $r$ value of .3 means that only 9 percent of the variance in $Y$ is linked with $X$.

determined both his or her educational level and occupational choice. If socioeconomic background, $Z$, as measured by low and high parental family income, were held constant, the relationship between educational level, $X$, and occupational choice, $Y$, might disappear. If we constructed separate tables for the two levels of socioeconomic background, the results might be as follows:

Table    2-2    **Hypothetical Data Showing No Relationship between Education and Occupational Choice When Socioeconomic Background is Controlled**

| Z: SOCIOECONOMIC BACKGROUND X: EDUCATION Y: OCCUPATIONAL CHOICE | Low-income Less than high school degree | High school degree and beyond | TOTAL |
|---|---|---|---|
| Blue-collar | 56 | 24 | 80 |
| White-collar | 14 | 6 | 20 |
| | 70 | 30 | 100 |

Table    2-3    **Hypothetical Data Showing No Relationship between Education and Occupational Choice When Socioeconomic Background Is Controlled**

| Z: SOCIOECONOMIC BACKGROUND X: EDUCATION Y: OCCUPATIONAL CHOICE | High-income Less than high school degree | High school degree and beyond | TOTAL |
|---|---|---|---|
| Blue-collar | 6 | 14 | 20 |
| White-collar | 24 | 56 | 80 |
| | 30 | 70 | 100 |

The first thing to notice about Tables 2-2 and 2-3 is that if respondents with low and high socioeconomic backgrounds were combined, the resulting totals would coincide exactly with those for the previous table. That is, the previous results have been differentiated further, or disaggregated, so as to *control* for socioeconomic or income background. Therefore, within the limits of this unrefined dichotomy, socioeconomic status has been *held constant* while other factors vary. The data indicate no relationship between educational level and occupational choice within either of the two subtables, since among low socioeconomic background respondents, 80 percent of both low- and high-educational level individuals have chosen blue-collar craft and trade occupations, whereas among the high-income group 80 percent of both educational groups have chosen white-collar professional, technical, or managerial occupations. With a control for socioeconomic background, the original relationship has disappeared.

One possible explanation, in this hypothetical case, is that the relationship between $X$ and $Y$ is what scientists term a *spurious* relationship. That is, under certain conditions it appears to be a causal relationship when actually it is not one. The variable $Z$ represents the control variable, socioeconomic background, which may be a common cause of both $X$ and $Y$. This can be diagrammed as:

Common sense would suggest that if this were so, then $Z$ ought to be more strongly related to $X$ and $Y$, than $X$ and $Y$ are to each other.[2] We must remember, however, that numerous other causal factors will be operating. If we assume that the aggregate effect of these variables produces random (chance) disturbances in both $X$ and $Y$, then according to this simple theoretical model their correlation can only be accounted for by $Z$. If $Z$ were held constant, there would be no reason to expect $X$ and $Y$ to be associated.

This very simple argument can be stated much more rigorously, but it is essentially sound as it is. In fact, in the hypothetical data provided, socioeconomic background is strongly related to educational level and also to occupational choice. Therefore, we have found a plausible alternative explanation by locating a variable $Z$, highly related to both $X$ and $Y$, which is assumed to be a common cause. We would, then, have to conclude that the relationship between $X$ and $Y$ is spurious and due to the influence of $Z$.

The investigator may want to escape this difficulty, but in one sense it is impossible to do so since a critic can always identify a possible source of spuriousness. In fact, this is illustrated by the perennial struggle between cancer researchers and cigarette manufacturers, the latter claiming that a solid proof of causation is lacking. It is important to realize that, strictly speaking, no proof of causation is ever possible, since an investigator can never guarantee that there is no variable producing a spurious relationship. This is another way of saying that there is no method for deciding that all possible causes have been identified and controlled. This generalization applies even to

2.    In this simple model it can be shown that the correlation $r_{xy}$ can be expected to equal the *product* of the two correlations $r_{xz}$ and $r_{yz}$. For instance, if $r_{xz}$ were .6, and $r_{yz}$ were .5, we would expect the correlation between $X$ and $Y$ to be approximately .3.

experimental designs and is a fundamental limitation of *all* scientific research. It must be clearly recognized if unresolvable disputes are to be understood and minimized.

Yet something needs to be done to convince the reasonable skeptic that the investigator has been able to identify a real cause of $Y$, not simply a correlate. The burden of proof is mainly on the investigator to explore as many plausible alternative explanations as is feasible, given the limitations imposed by the design and methods within which the research is carried out. The competent social scientist is well aware of this problem, and careful research will always involve controls on numerous possible sources of spuriousness. Even so, the persistent critic may discover still another variable, at which point the burden of proof is on the skeptic to carry out a further study, control for this variable, and see if the original relationship can be reduced to zero. If it can be, the conclusions have to be revised.

This emphasizes the tentative nature of all theory and explanation, and justifies the cautious nature of research conclusions, a caution that is at times very exasperating to the student, researcher, consumer, and utilizer of research. Nevertheless, responsible research and interpretation refines explanation and produces increasingly more trustworthy theory on which to base continuing research activities.

If the kind of three-variable theoretical model provided in the illustration could be used as a realistic model, life would be relatively painless for the social scientist. Unfortunately a number of complications introduce further ambiguities and create a need for more technical knowledge. A few of these complications are now discussed, in order to explain the need for complex theory and statistical expertise.

### Alternative Models

Even in the three-variable model just illustrated, an alternative explanation can account equally well for the same empirical data given in the previous tables. Instead of causing both $X$ and $Y$, $Z$ may be an *intervening causal link* between them. That is, $X$ may cause $Z$, which in turn causes $Y$, as follows:

$$X \rightarrow Z \rightarrow Y$$

If $Z$ stands between $X$ and $Y$ in a causal sequence, it should be more highly correlated with both $X$ and $Y$ than $X$ and $Y$ are with one another.

For example, if we are studying the relationship between educational levels ($X$), occupational choices ($Y$), and employers' selections ($Z$) among job applicants based on their educational levels, these selections have to be viewed as an influence coming later in the temporal sequence of potential influences on occupational choice than does educational level. Employers' selections, then, represent the variable that intervenes between educational level and occupational choice. Educational level, in this context, can be understood more accurately as an *indirect cause* of occupational choice, mediated by the effect of employers' selections.

It can be shown, using rigorous methods, that if other potential causal factors have a net or aggregate random effect, then in both this and the previous example, controlling for $Z$ will produce a zero relationship between $X$ and $Y$. That is, the empirical results in the case of both models are the same. That is why it is important that for any variable $Z$ we must have a theory explaining the *direction* of the relationship between $X$ and $Z$. In models with multiple variables, the same basic principle applies. Alternative explanations involving identical variables can explain a particular set of data equally effectively.

This complication has significant practical as well as theoretical implications, particularly for policy. In the case of the first model, in which $X$ and $Y$ are related spuriously due to the influence of $Z$, policy directed toward changing $X$ would have no impact on $Y$ unless $Z$ were also changed. In the alternative model illustrated here, since $X$ causes $Z$, a change in $X$ would affect $Z$, which in turn would affect $Y$. Clearly, the policy strategies flowing from these two alternative explanations would be substantially different.

A safe generalization to make is that there will always be more than one explanation for any specific phenomenon, as well as for each set of data resulting from research. Therefore it is necessary to use as wide a range of information as possible in developing explanatory models on which research can be based. If researchers can infer time sequences among key variables, as well as correlations between them, they are in a better position to choose among alternative explanations of the data. Likewise, theoretical models provide better guides if both temporal and association linkages are proposed for investigation, based on the prior knowledge base available on the particular phenomenon to be studied. Such models direct the collection of data at more than one point in time, a process that should be followed if at all possible.

### Additional Variables

A second kind of complication arises if there are two (or more) sources of spuriousness. To illustrate with the previous variables, let us assume there is a positive relationship between educational level, $X$, and occupational choice, $Y$, and that this relationship may be due to *two* common causes, ethnic status, $W$, and socioeconomic background, $Z$. That is, *both* $W$ and $Z$ are sources of spuriousness in explaining the relationship between $X$ and $Y$:

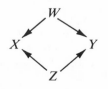

In order to sort out these relationships, it would be necessary to control *simultaneously* for ethnic status and socioeconomic background. To introduce such controls, a series of four tables would need to be constructed, one each for (1) minority individuals with low socioeconomic background, (2) minority individuals with high socioeconomic background, (3) nonminority individuals with low socioeconomic background and (4) nonminority individuals with high socioeconomic background. If there were five ethnic statuses and two socioeconomic levels, this would require ten separate tables, each involving a different subcategory combination of ethnic status and socioeconomic background.

This principle can be extended to any number of control variables. If there were four separate sources of spuriousness, then in order to hold all of these constant simultaneously there would have to be a separate table for each *combination* of categories of the control variables. For example, if two additional control variables were sex and age, there would have to be a separate table for each of the categories of sex and age—e.g., one table including only young, nonminority males with low socioeconomic background, a second including only young, nonminority females with low socioeconomic background, and so on.

This process of controlling variables becomes cumbersome and difficult. But more important, a point will be reached where there are no longer sufficient numbers of individuals (cases) in each table. For example, with five ethnic statuses, two socioeconomic levels, two sexes, and two age groups, there would have to be forty separate tables. If the researcher had only two hundred cases in his or her study to begin with, this would mean an average of only five cases per table! One very important implication is that if one suspects that a large number of controls will be needed, one will have to begin with a very large sample. Fortunately there are alternative, more complex ways of controlling for many variables at once, but these also involve certain kinds of simplifying assumptions. Reality is remarkably complex, therefore the analysis of that reality must inevitably be so.

### Correlated Independent Variables

A third kind of complication occurs in situations where a number of the variables thought to be determinants or causes of another variable are themselves highly intercorrelated. In the case of the phenomenon of poverty, low educational levels, low incomes, high rates of unemployment, inadequate housing, and insufficient physical and mental health care may *all* be possible sources of another variable, such as political unrest. How can the separate effects of each variable be inferred?

The major advantage of experimental designs, to be discussed in Chapter 4, is that several causal factors can be independently manipulated so that their separate effects are not confounded together. But in the real world they *are* found together, even though their correlations may not be perfect.

There may be a small number of individuals with deprived educational backgrounds who have high incomes, and a small proportion of the unemployed who have adequate health care. This fact makes it possible to separate out their individual effects, provided the samples of cases are very large and provided very good measures can be obtained for each variable. But this necessitates a much more complex kind of statistical analysis. Given the limitations of any particular research project, it is often impossible to separate the component effects of individual variables with any degree of confidence. In these instances, they must be treated as a single "syndrome," such as "poverty," or as a cluster of variables that must be considered all at once.

Theoretical models intended to guide research on such issues must clearly describe what variables are subsumed under a particular category, and what assumptions are being made about their interrelationships. Using well-defined models of this kind, and pursuing research within an experimental design if possible, the researcher may be able to gain insights that can be applied to the more complex situations found in the real environment.

### Measurement Errors

A fourth kind of complication is introduced by the presence of measurement errors, which in the social sciences are often quite large. As already implied, the more highly intercorrelated the causal variables, the more serious the distortions produced by measurement errors. In effect, measurement errors introduce additional unknowns into the testing situation; and where the nature and extent of errors in the evidence used to identify variables remain undetected or unknown, the consequences are very serious. In the poverty example, if the researcher selected as the *only* measure of adequate health care the number of recorded visits to a doctor within a specified time period, it is probable that other kinds of critical evidence of health care provision will remain unknown and unmeasured, consequently distorting the health care data used in correlating that variable with education, income, or other variables.

In relatively simple situations, it is possible to anticipate and describe what kinds of adverse effects particular forms of measurement errors are likely to have. For example, in the first spurious situation $Z$ was assumed to be a common cause of both $X$ and $Y$. If there is a random measurement error in $Z$, then the relationship between $X$ and $Y$ will not disappear if $Z$ is controlled. This is because $Z$ is only imperfectly controlled, due to the investigator's uncertain knowledge of the "true" values (indicators or measures) of $Z$.

This problem of evaluating the effects of measurement error is extremely complex, and the consequences are not always clear. Without resolving such measurement problems to some degree, definitive studies simply cannot be carried out. In a very real sense, the advancement of science depends not only on well-conceived theoretical models but on the adequacy with which the variables in those models are defined for data collection purposes. This issue will be discussed more thoroughly in the next chapter.

### Interaction Effects

A fifth complication in constructing and applying explanatory models in research is the problem of *interaction effects*. Such effects are what statisticians refer to as the nonadditive effects of unusual combinations of variables. As "first approximations," the effects of several variables may be taken as additive. For example, if researchers are trying to explain the effects of age, sex, ethnic status, and education on income levels, they might simply add the possible separate effects of these variables. It might be that a constant (nonvariable) increment in income level could be added for the presence of each of the other variables, irrespective of educational level: perhaps $2,000 in income for being male, $1,500 for being middle-aged, and $1,000 for being white. An additional constant, perhaps $500, might be added for the effect of each year of education—i.e., the same constant amount for males and females, young and old, white and nonwhite. Conversely, this could be viewed as subtracting separate constants from income levels for being young, female, black, and poorly educated. The effect of a number of causal variables can be illustrated as:

$$\text{Income} = \text{Constant} + \text{Sex Effect} + \text{Age Effect} + \text{Ethnic Effect} + \text{Education Effect}$$

where the appropriate constants, or unchanging increments, would need to be substituted for each of the variables on the right side of the equation. This, however, is not what is meant by interaction effects.

Several possible results of research focused on the relationship between these variables must be considered. One potential finding might be the existence of relatively small differences between the incomes of whites and nonwhites at low educational levels, but rather large ones at the higher levels. Another finding might be that differences between the incomes of white and nonwhite women were much smaller than those for men. A third might be that education made a significantly larger difference for the incomes of men than for women. If any of these were the research outcomes, then the simple model shown in the previous equation would not apply.

The reason would lie in the more complicated interactive effects of sex, age, ethnic status, and education on income—effects that would differ from those produced by simply adding the separate effects. The researchers in this last case could not assume a simple relationship between education and income, but would need to refer specifically to the sex, age, and ethnic status of the individuals studied. That is, we might have four different relationships between education and income, one each for white males, nonwhite males,

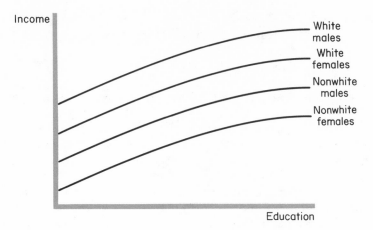

**Figure 2-2** Parallel Curves Showing Additive Effects of Sex, Race, and Education on Income

white females, and nonwhite females. The relationships and their explanation would therefore have to be conceived in much more complex terms. Had the relationships been simpler, the result could have been represented by a series of parallel curves, as illustrated in Figure 2-2. When the curves are parallel, there is always a constant difference or increment between any two curves, for example, between those for white and nonwhite males. However, with an interactive effect present, the relationships might look like those in Figure 2-3.

It is clear that many phenomena in the social environment involve relationships in which the joint effects of several variables are extremely complicated, and where explanations that ignore the plausibility of interactive effects can be very misleading. This problem will be discussed again in Chapter 4.

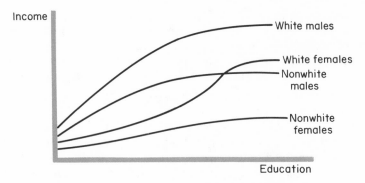

**Figure 2-3** Nonparallel Curves Showing Interactive or Nonadditive Effects of Sex, Race, and Education on Income

## Reciprocal Causation

A sixth complication arises whenever there is *reciprocal causation,* or influences among the important variables that act in both directions. This occurs frequently in real life situations, though it often involves a time lag. In the case of poverty, we assume that low levels of education, occupation, and income in one generation tend to produce low motivation and numerous school dropouts in the next generation, which in turn tends to affect the jobs and income the second generation will receive, and so on through successive generations. It would not be particularly difficult to handle this kind of situation analytically, but practically speaking one cannot draw neat generational distinctions when aggregate populations are concerned. Exactly who is in what generation? There will be a continuous distribution of ages, and therefore it is only within individual families that one can speak in terms of distinct generations.

Whenever the researcher allows for the possibility of reciprocal causation, whereby $X$ can affect $Y$ and $Y$ also affect $X$, the basic difficulty is that there are simply too many unknown parameters or weights, none of which can be adequately estimated from the data available. The main question becomes one of deciding whether $X$ has a bigger impact on $Y$ or $Y$ on $X$.

A global example would be the controversy over competing "antiwar" strategies whose applications likely have a strong effect on one another in preventing or triggering the use of force. For example, the first nation may decide to increase its level of military preparedness for various reasons. A second nation may respond by increasing its own level of weaponry, leading to another increase in the first nation's outlay for arms, and so on until war may become inevitable. Even if there is a time lag between the application of the strategies, the chicken and egg problem persists, since it is difficult to separate out the extent to which the first strategy influenced the development of the second, or the second reduced or escalated the first.

The resolution of this kind of problem requires sophisticated *estimation procedures,* developed largely by statisticians and economists to estimate the relative influence of variables considered to have a complex reciprocal effect on each other. The first of these procedures requires the collection of *time-series data,* data on the same individuals over a reasonably prolonged period of time. Economists are fortunate that income, cost, and production data are available on a regular basis. These data are reasonably well standardized across businesses and industries, since many items can be compared in terms of dollars (e.g., labor costs or sales prices) or can be counted easily (e.g., numbers of automobiles produced).

However, time-series data can also be gathered in other studies, such as small-group experiments. For example, in a study of the effects of sleep deprivation, the observer may take a frequency count of instances of frustration and acts of aggression every fifteen minutes, or measures of these variables may be taken during regular weekly sessions. Many kinds of data are expensive to collect, however, and being asked the same questions time and again may also affect research results. *Panel studies,* in which the same respondent is interviewed a number of times at prescribed intervals, is one device used in what is termed *survey research.* Surveys will be discussed briefly in the next chapter.

A second kind of resolution involves finding additional causes of the reciprocally related variables—that is, causes that are not themselves in any way dependent on the variables in question. A favorite example cited by economists is rainfall. Wheat yields and therefore prices are clearly dependent on rainfall, but rainfall is not considered dependent on economic variables. Even this example is problematic, however, since as humans gain increasing control over their environment there will be fewer of these truly independent variables. At some future point, rainfall may become increasingly dependent on farmers' attitudes and agricultural technology, as it has with the use of cloud-seeding techniques.

Not only must researchers identify the variables that are genuinely independent, they must also make explicit certain *a priori* (and usually untestable) assumptions with respect to *which* of these independent variables influence (or cause) specific dependent variables. Researchers must avoid the possibility that every independent variable affects every dependent variable directly, for they will again have too many unknowns. They must introduce additional independent variables selectively, in order to resolve the problem of the direction of cause and effect. For example, the economist must assume that rainfall affects agricultural yields and therefore the supply of these products, while assuming that it does not directly affect customers' preferences for these products. If these assumptions were unrealistic, the researcher would have to find other independent variables to accomplish the same goal.

This brief summary of factors that complicate the development of explanatory models, and therefore interfere with making valid inferences from data collected through research, is meant to convey the complexity of theory and research and the ultimate need for large-scale, long-term research projects utilizing the most sophisticated models, technical designs, and methods available.

## THE DEVELOPMENT OF SYSTEMATIC THEORY

In view of this complexity, and the literally thousands of research issues in which the social scientist is likely to become interested or is requested to study, a major challenge is how to develop reasonable guidelines for selecting among the numerous variables and problems these issues involve. Is there any hope that an extremely large number of miscellaneous facts can be integrated into a small number of rather coherent sets of relationships? We are still not very far along in achieving this objective. Nevertheless, social scientists are well aware of the need for sound theory that will integrate research findings, provide the necessary guidelines, and make comparative analyses simpler. And there is significant movement in that direction.

For example, in sociology there have been a number of "grand theorists," the most prominent of whom was Talcott Parsons of Harvard. These theorists have made major contributions in resolving the difficult problem of integrating the field. Researchers have generally found, however, that the primary value of these theories has been in providing *sensitizing concepts,* or ideas that alert the investigator to the possible importance of a given set of variables. For instance, the concept of "role" is used to sensitize the sociologist to look for certain regularized patterns of behavior that are associated with particular positions, but are relatively independent of the specific individuals who happen to be occupying these positions at any one time. But the grand theorists have provided us with relatively few *specific propositions* that are sufficiently precise to yield testable hypotheses.

Robert Merton, a student of Parsons, was one of the first sociologists to take a point of view, now widely accepted, that our greatest need is for ***theories of the middle range.*** The intent of these theories is to explain particular kinds of phenomena with sufficient clarity and concreteness to imply a set of interrelated hypotheses that can then be applied to several apparently diverse phenomena.[3] There are a number of theoretical discussions of large-scale organizations and bureaucratic behavior, for example, that are meant to account for patterns in many different kinds of organizations: businesses, corporations, labor unions, churches, political parties, prisons, and so on. Yet these frameworks are not designed to account for all the behavior of individuals, or for societal development, or for international conflict. Their objectives and limitations are relatively narrow and their propositions are reasonably specific.

One of the greatest needs in the social sciences is for middle-range theories that can suggest in very specific ways how findings about particular phenomena can be used to draw inferences about other phenomena. There are myriad forms of "deviance," for example, only a few of which are socially defined as serious enough to come to the attention of the public, such as crime, suicide, drug addiction, or overt rebellion. Suppose the social scientists studying burglary had to develop a theory of burglary completely independently of a theory used to account for homicide. Given the large number of explanatory variables that might be used in each case, this would be an extremely wasteful procedure. It would be preferable to have a theory that accounted for both burglary and homicide, and that also explained suicide as

---

3.  This point of view is elaborated in Robert K. Merton, *Social Theory and Social Structure,* rev. ed. (New York: The Free Press of Glencoe, 1968).

well. In fact, it would be desirable to have a general explanation for all forms of social deviance.

But while such a general theory might be desirable, it may not be realistic to suppose that it would adequately explain all forms of deviance, just as a theoretical explanation of "disease" would be of little value to the practicing physician. One runs the risk that an extremely general explanation, if in fact "true," will be so vague or abstract that it will not make any really specific predictions that are capable of being tested by empirical research. For example, one might explain all deviance in terms of parental rejection, but such a theory would not specify the mechanisms that produce one form of deviance rather than another, nor would it account for varying degrees of deviance. What general theories do accomplish is that critical sensitizing function. They may suggest that the investigator look for parental rejection as a first step in the analysis.

Many such general explanations have a good deal of popular appeal because of their simplicity. All we need to do to prevent deviance is to socialize parents better! And being nebulous, these theories can be used to account ex post facto for almost any form of deviance that may occur. They may be modified, elaborated, and made seemingly more technical as the occasion demands. But their predictive power may be very weak. The problem is to make them more specific by spelling out very explicitly what they imply under carefully defined conditions. This will produce a number of *subtheories of the middle range*.

Inherent within any scientific field is that awesome strain between the need for relatively simple general explanations and the need for more specific theories of a narrower range of applicability. There will always be differences of opinion among scientists and others as to what priorities are to be developed between and within these two levels of theory. Most social scientists would probably agree that both levels are important and that each supports the other, but there will be much less consensus about how much time and energy should be devoted to each. In many social science fields, for example, much more effort is being expended on the more specific formulations, leaving a considerable gap between the most general sociological theories and the actual research being carried out.

You may wonder at this point why scientists cannot dispense with theories altogether and simply give attention to concrete problems as they surface, such as urban youth unemployment, sexism in health care, the energy crisis, or population problems. This raises the fundamental question of the purpose of science, apart from addressing issues of immediate concern to one or another constituency or special interest group in society. In the purer sense, science rests on intellectual curiosity and the appreciation of knowledge for its own sake. It stresses objectivity in applying the scientific method to generic research questions. Less central to this strictly scientific perspective is a concern with the application of one's theories and empirical findings to real-life issues, and with the obligations social scientists have to the development of social policy and the resolution of social problems.

In this context, one of the answers to why we need theories is that they are critical to the objective pursuit of cumulative knowledge. Theories also increase the usefulness of diverse research findings so that they have meaning for more than the one problem area to which they may be most immediately relevant. Most social scientists are sensitive to the philosophical and ethical problems posed by their own values and decisions with respect to what kinds of research are appropriate to pursue, and many firmly believe their work should contribute to the prevention and resolution of social problems. The majority also continue to believe that general theory and basic research—i.e., theory and research that are not *necessarily* immediately applicable to an existing issue or problem in the pragmatic world—are absolutely essential to the development of our knowledge of social phenomena. This is true even when the ultimate objective is to increase the level of awareness and knowledge about particular contemporary social problems. Why should this conviction be so strong?

The difficulty with applied research—which gives primary attention to pragmatic questions—is that the problems studied change rapidly, so rapidly that researchers are unable to study them thoroughly. By the time they have conducted a comprehensive study of one phenomenon, it may have given way to another. It may take so long to conduct the research that the problem will have either disappeared or been obscured or forgotten. Even if the phenomenon has not changed completely, many of the specifics may change with sufficient rapidity that by the time the research report has been made available the findings will no longer accurately describe the true state of affairs.

Prior study of the complicated causal relationships between specific social problems is often undertaken in order to develop reasonable alternative solutions on the basis of which action options can be recommended. This approach, however, is sometimes criticized by activist-oriented social scientists who feel this slower approach is exploited by those opposing social change. Certainly this process is often so motivated and sometimes does serve such a function. However, careful study of a social problem within a general theoretical framework is critical to the development of the effective action alternatives activists seek. The resulting action options may be ill-advised or entirely too dated if the research is not approached as a basic long-term commitment to the search for underlying complex causes and effects.

Scientists cannot afford to be satisfied with theories that consist of such dated relationships, except as admissions of honest ignorance of the true causal mechanisms at work. Astronomical laws that merely described the positions of specific bodies—say, the planets of the solar system—would not be very useful unless these positions were repeated with a high degree of regularity. Astronomers are fortunate that such a high degree of regularity does in fact occur, though the movements of phenomena they study (such as distant stars) are so imperceptible, relative to the times between observations, that other laws are necessary to predict their long-term behavior. The fact that such extreme regularities do not occur in the social realm has led many observers to the pessimistic conclusion that the scientific study of human beings is impossible.

The most useful scientific laws, then, are those that do not refer directly to concrete events (e.g., the position of Venus at 8:05 P.M., July 1, 1982), but are instead phrased more generally in the form of "if-then" statements. *If a body is moving with a particular velocity and momentum in a specified gravitational field, then its position can be expected to change according to some specified law.* If one then wants to refer to a particular historical event, such as the position of Venus on a given day, this general law can be applied to the concrete case. In addition to the law itself, however, it will be necessary to supply some concrete facts about the mass and present velocity of Venus and its present position in relation to the sun and other planets. It will also be necessary to make certain simplifying assumptions about the lack of disturbances from outside factors (e.g., nearby stars).

This example illustrates the important point that *a precisely formulated general law,* plus some *assumptions about neglected factors or influences,* plus *a set of facts* that describe a particular phenomenon may actually be used to forecast what will happen. In the absence of the law, a less satisfactory forecast may be made by extrapolating past and present behavior into the future. This latter kind of forecast may be a very good one if there are no important changes in any of the variables. For example, the researcher might take the number of major organized labor strikes in the 1980s and obtain an estimate five years into the future, under the assumption that whatever the causes of the strikes, they will continue to operate as they have before. This does not take into account the effect of inflationary factors in the 1980s versus five years later, or other variables explanatory of labor-management positions affecting strike action. And of course, it gives us no insights as to how the number of strikes may be reduced or how the fundamental causes may be identified and manipulated.

Therefore one of the most serious and difficult problems confronting the social scientist is that of developing reasonably general theories or laws of social behavior that are not so restricted with respect to time and place that they can be applied only under very limited circumstances. The more restrictive the law, the less likely it will remain appropriate for use in practical situations, and its implications continually tested.

Even if a general theory about the behavior of members of an unusual religious colony could be constructed and tested, and even if it predicted their behavior extremely well, its usefulness would disappear with the last member of the sect. Perhaps later a similar variety of this phenomenon might reappear, in which case the theory might again be applied with minor modifications. But clearly a theory restricted to this single type of religious behavior will be useful only to the extent that the phenomenon persists. The theory would contribute much more to our knowledge of such phenomena if it could be generalized to include, for example, forms of behavior characteristic of a large number of social movements. But this more general formulation would undoubtedly be less detailed and predictions based on it would be much less precise.

So we have a peculiar kind of dilemma in many of the social sciences because the phenomena we study are often not as persistent and regular—relative to the time it takes to study them—as those in some of the physical sciences. Yet many social phenomena appear to be all too persistent: wars, prejudice and discrimination, poverty, crime, many kinds of interpersonal conflict, and so on. Many less "problematic" phenomena are also persistent, such as the formation of close friendship groups, authority relationships within bureaucratic organizations, or division of labor patterns within families. It would seem possible to develop reasonably specific theories about these phenomena, even in the absence of highly general laws. But in the case of the more fleeting phenomena, we may have to rely on general theories with less specific predictive value.

If general laws of human behavior are to be found, they will undoubtedly have to be complex if they are to apply to a wide range of specific phenomena. For example, simple statements such as "the greater $X$, the greater $Y$" will have to be modified by spelling out the conditions under which the statements can be applied. A good deal of attention must also be given to the question of exactly what is to be included as $X$ or as $Y$.

To illustrate in terms of dominant-subordinate relationships, it would certainly be useful if we could explain many different forms of dominance relationships in terms of a single theory of power. For example, what is there in common between male-female, parent-child, white-black, criminal-noncriminal, or large nation-small nation relationships? Can we spell out the conditions under which increasing punishment by the dominant party will lead to increased resistance by the subordinate party, as contrasted with the conditions under which the subordinate party will yield? If a really adequate theory existed, it could be applied to some new power relationship not yet systematically studied.

But as the theory is made more general, the concepts or variables in that theory become much more abstract and difficult to measure. It may not be too difficult to specify a set of conditions that affect relationships between whites and minorities in the United States in a particular decade, but can our conceptualization of these conditions be broadened to apply to relationships among nations or between husbands and wives? Are there any *general principles* that serve as useful guidelines? Philosophers of science have given a good deal of thought to this kind of question on a very abstract level, but there are very few useful rules social scientists can follow in constructing specific theories that lead in some systematic way to more general explanations. Despite the constraints, however, the progressive movement of theoretical and empirical work toward formulating general laws remains a significant scientific goal.

## THE RELATIONSHIP
## BETWEEN THEORY AND MEASUREMENT

The complexity of theoretical tasks, and the necessity to perform them, should now be clearer. An explanatory model is essential for carrying out competent research. It is unproductive for the researcher to pursue other steps in the research process without a theoretical basis, however sparse or full, simple or complicated. If the nature of the relationships among influential variables is not well specified, the ideas flowing from the research will have no frame of reference. However, the drama of the research process only *begins* with an adequate explanation. What must concern the researcher next?

One of the reasons for the difficulties in developing general principles and laws is that problems of measurement place serious limitations on this process. Suppose the researcher's ultimate purpose is to generalize findings about prejudice: For example, how can prejudice toward women, ethnic minorities, elected officials, sexual minorities and others be measured so that the researcher can confidently conclude that the measures being used were all reflecting the same kind of generic attitude pattern? The question then becomes how one measures the major explanatory variables in order to gather valid data for analysis and interpretation. While theory requires us to move up the abstraction ladder in our thinking, measurement demands that we apply the same expertise in moving down. Each direction presents its own special challenges. If measurement issues are not properly addressed and problems solved, the value of the theoretical model is seriously compromised.

# CHAPTER 3
# MEASUREMENT

We think in generalities, we live in detail.

While theory is the first concern of the social researcher, measurement is of tremendous importance both to theory and to the general development of the social sciences. Why is measurement so significant?

*Measurement* is the process through which explanatory variables are more specifically defined. This procedure of progressive definition, leading to increasingly more precise descriptions of variables, forms the basis for data collection and analysis, and ultimately for the interpretation of results and their use. It ensures that the data collected will reflect as accurately as possible the characteristics of the major variables in the theoretical explanation. Therefore, the development of valid indices, or *measures* of variables (the end products of the measurement process), is critical to research and represents one of its most complex aspects.

The competence of research activities is strongly affected by the clarity and preciseness with which the researcher is able to translate the abstract meaning of the key variables within a theoretical framework into *operational definitions,* or practical, pragmatic, explicit descriptions that guide the search for information. In this context, theory and measurement are interdependent elements of research.

Historically, there has been a persistent neglect in social research of the many problems and stimulating possibilities that the measurement process involves. The important relationship between explanation and measurement, a central issue in the integration of theory and research, has not always been given sufficient priority. The complexity and sometimes perplexing intricacy of measurement issues have been poorly understood. Naming, classifying, and defining what an abstract theoretical concept "stands for" are difficult procedures and require a series of steps, through which the abstract meaning of a variable is systematically broken down into progressively more concrete tangible meanings that permit the direct collection of valid data. The simplest measure of the most easily defined variable in an explanation can be challenged in terms of whether it accurately reflects the "real" qualities of the phenomenon the researcher says is being studied. The researcher needs to select evidence that is widely agreed upon, and that can be explained clearly and precisely so that it is unmistakable to other researchers what entity is being identified. The data ultimately assembled will then have relevance for the researcher's original set of propositions.

Several of the pitfalls in this process are: (1) selecting measures that are overly simplistic, (2) narrowing the meaning of the abstract concept by the choice of too few measures or indices, and (3) introducing inconsistencies in meaning as one moves from theory to specific measures.

To illustrate these problems, let us assume the researcher is interested in studying the relationship between family cohesiveness and the family authority structure. These are quite abstract but fascinating concepts that the researcher expects will contribute to knowledge about family life. Assume also that the researcher, for undetermined reasons, proposes that the more authoritarian the structure of decision making, the more cohesive the family, hoping perhaps to refute this proposition with the data collected. Assume further that the researcher selects "the incidence of divorce" as the index of cohesiveness, and the question, "who makes the primary decision on major family purchases?" as the sole measure of authority structure.

What alternative sources of evidence about these variables may this researcher be leaving out, in using such simple indicators of these complex concepts? Certainly there are many other important potential indices of cohesiveness, such as degree of marital and parent-child conflict, incidence of marital and parent-child separations, quality of communication patterns, or styles of problem resolution. Likewise, family authority structure can be measured across a number of critical areas of decision, and from evidence other than decision making. In moving from abstract meanings of the central concepts to specific ways of identifying evidence of their presence, the researcher has excluded important possibilities and forced unwarranted assumptions about the consistency of meaning between the general definitions and the highly selective choices of specific definitions. If the data were to suggest that families characterized by rigid domination of purchasing decisions by a single member are the most cohesive, what biases would be expressed in these findings, and how could the researcher ever fully compensate for the errors these biases bring to the interpretation of the data?

A great deal of research unfortunately suffers from the lack of multiple diverse measures that appropriately represent the variables of interest. Much research is constrained by a benign neglect of the steps in the definitional process. In the example, the abundant range of measurement possibilities has been lost to the research process and cannot be easily retrieved.

This hypothetical case suggests some of the implications of measurement. A good theory can be promptly compromised or greatly enhanced through this process. Also, the way in which measurement alternatives are identified and selected, and measurement problems anticipated and resolved, influences the development, choice, and use of frameworks that guide the researcher in deciding what strategies and techniques are most appropriate to those frameworks. In affecting the validity of research results, the measurement process also has repercussions for the ongoing revision and improvement of theory.

One reason why accurate measurement is necessary is that if the supposed causes of a phenomenon such as delinquency or discrimination are highly intercorrelated, it becomes technically impossible to separate out their component effects without accurate measures. In general, the more highly interrelated variables are, the more accurate our measures of each must be. Even where one or two important variables have been correctly identified and isolated, accurate measurement may be necessary in order to refine the analysis beyond the common-sense level. For example, we often hear the assertion that the higher the concentration of nonwhites within a given area, the greater the discrimination found. But does this imply a simple linear, or straight-line relationship between a particular kind of discrimination and minority percentage? Or is a more complex, nonlinear relationship more appropriate? If nonlinear, exactly what kind of curve will work best? Obviously the better the measurement of both variables, the more precise we can be about the relationships.

Another very important reason why measurement needs to be improved is that measurement considerations often enable us to clarify our theoretical thinking and to suggest new variables. Scientists have often assumed, prior to actual attempts to measure their variables, that they understand the nature of a phenomenon well because they have experienced it directly. For instance, all researchers have a basic understanding of what "prejudice" is. But as soon as they begin to measure it quantitatively, as in a paper-and-pencil test of attitudes, they must deal with critics who object that "true" prejudice cannot be measured by such a simple technique. Its essence cannot be identified easily. If, however, these critics are questioned as to exactly what this "true" essence is, they will usually find it almost impossible to describe exactly what they mean. They may construct their own paper-and-pencil test, in which case an argument is likely to occur as to which test is the "best" measure of prejudice, the basic qualities of which are again thought to be understood.

This is how science must proceed. When one attempts to spell out the specific procedures to be used in the measurement process (that is, the specific questions one will ask), one may discover that different persons have different conceptions of what a variable such as "prejudice" is meant to convey. As data are actually collected, it may also become evident that responses to the questions do not mesh as had been originally expected. For example, it is certainly possible that men who use unfavorable stereotypes about women's traits—e.g., passive, dependent, emotional— do not necessarily believe that women should be discriminated against in the workplace. In effect, the data may lead one to infer several distinct dimensions or aspects of prejudice that are not very highly intercorrelated. This means that prejudice should not be studied as though it were a single variable. There may be different kinds of prejudice that have very different implications for theories of discrimination. This turns out, in fact, to be the case. The important general point, however, is that careful attention to measurement may force a clarification of one's basic ideas and concepts, and therefore of one's theories.

## LEVELS OF MEASUREMENT

Ordinarily when we think about measurement, we visualize measuring the length of a table, using a stopwatch to time a runner, or looking at a thermometer to infer temperature. We are aware that some measurement procedures are much more accurate than others, and we recognize that many measures are indirect. Before we focus on the indirectness of measurement in both the natural and the social sciences, we must first consider what we shall refer to as distinct *levels* of measurement. We may think of these levels as involving differing degrees of precision, although in actuality the issues that we encounter in distinguishing among these levels are much more subtle than this simple distinction implies.

Another approach to measurement levels is to think of them as representing different levels of sophistication in measurement *procedures,* each level justifying a different and more complex kind of statistical operation. To be more specific, let us begin with the simplest level of measurement, the ***nominal scale.***

### Nominal Scales

Measurement involves classification. If we can classify individuals into mutually exclusive and exhaustive categories, then it is possible to count cases and to determine the degree to which one category predicts to another. For example, if adults can be classified as "Protestants," "Catholics," "Jews," and "Others," and also as "Republicans," "Democrats," "Independents," and "Others," they can then be cross-tabulated as follows in Table 3-1:

Table 3-1    Hypothetical Data Showing a Relationship between Religious
Denomination and Political Party Preference

| | PROTESTANTS | CATHOLICS | JEWS | OTHERS | TOTAL |
|---|---|---|---|---|---|
| Republicans | 500 | 100 | 50 | 30 | 680 |
| Democrats | 300 | 300 | 200 | 40 | 840 |
| Independents | 100 | 80 | 100 | 20 | 300 |
| Others | 100 | 20 | 50 | 10 | 180 |
| Total | 1000 | 500 | 400 | 100 | 2000 |

There is no ordering necessarily implied in such classifications. One could interchange two columns or rows without making any difference. Sometimes these groupings may be used in such a way as to imply an ordering, however. For example, if political party were taken as an indicator of political liberalism, we might wish to insert the Independents between the Republicans and Democrats, leaving the "Other" category as a residual grouping including communists, socialists, vegetarians, and persons who are completely nonpolitical. But if no ordering is implied, these simple classifications are commonly referred to as *nominal scales,* since we have done nothing else than give a *name* to the category without implying any other qualities.

There are, of course, many ways that individuals may be categorized, but only a few of these will be practically or theoretically useful. In the above example we have categorized persons by religious denomination because we believe that domination will be related to some other basis for classification, such as political preference. If this in fact turns out to be the case, as is true in Table 3-1, then we may make statements to the effect that Protestants are more likely to be Republicans than are either Catholics or Jews. This may be a research finding, or it may be predicted in advance of data collection and be tested as an hypothesis. In a preliminary study that intends mainly to explore an issue, investigators may be left with a definite impression that relatively more people of one kind (e.g., Protestants) are also likely to be classified as something else (e.g., Republicans), but they may not have had the opportunity to do the actual counting. In a descriptive survey, on the other hand, the actual numerical data may have been obtained and the findings displayed in tables similar to the one above.

### Ordinal Scales

People are often relatively easy to categorize, and in fact they place each other into categories all the time. Mr. Martin may be a palmist, a convert to an obscure religious sect, a father, a grandfather, a member of the Montesano Jogging Club, and a resident of the state penitentiary. These are measurable characteristics. A much more difficult task, however, is finding useful ways of ordering these classes based on meaningful criteria. For example, most Americans freely admit that occupations can be roughly ranked according to their prestige, though there may be minor disagreements, and certain kinds of occupations will be difficult to place. Therefore a person may be given an occupational prestige score that places that person on a continuum from high to low (or good to bad, skilled to unskilled, and so forth). If this is possible, the resulting scale is usually referred to as an *ordinal scale.*

The defining characteristic of an ordinal scale lies in what is called its transitive property: if $A$ is greater than $B$ (written $A > B$), and $B$ greater than $C$, then $A$ must be greater than $C$. If this does not hold for all individuals, then we do not have a legitimate ordinal scale. We know of situations in sports where $A$ can beat $B$, $B$ can beat $C$, but yet $C$ can beat $A$. In such instances we might intuitively suspect that there is more than one dimension involved, and we cannot obtain a unique ordering or ranking.

In many instances, social scientists must settle for rather crude ordinal scales in which there are numerous ties. They may have roughly divided families into six social classes, which they may have termed the "lower-lower," the "upper-lower," the "lower-middle," the "upper-middle," the "lower-upper," and the "upper-upper." Clearly, a prestige ordering is implied in this terminology, but there will be large numbers of individuals who are treated as being tied and are placed in the same class. Whenever such ties occur, there is always the question of whether they are really ties or whether they merely reflect the crudity of the measuring instrument. Usually it is the latter. Few researchers believe that they can find a fixed number of distinct social classes composed of completely homogeneous (or tied) individuals. They recognize that there is a continuous gradation of statuses and that they have arbitrarily decided to use six rather than some other number of classes.

### Interval and Ratio Scales

At times it is possible to utilize a standard unit of measure, such as the pound, meter, second, or dollar, thus making it possible to speak about the numerical sizes of the differences among scores. These kinds of measures are most common in the physical sciences, but there are some available to the social scientist as well. An obvious one is the monetary unit. Time may also be used as the basis of such a unit, as for example the number of years of formal schooling or the amount of time spent watching TV. Whenever social scientists compare communities, the relative numbers of certain types of people can be used as the basis of the unit. Cities may be contrasted with respect to relative numbers of nonwhites or the percentage of the labor force in manufacturing.

When such objective units exist, it becomes possible to compare differences. For example, if $A$'s income is \$20,000, if $B$'s is \$14,000, and $C$'s is \$8,000, we can say that $B$'s income is halfway between $A$'s and $C$'s, or equivalently that if there were another person with the same income as $B$'s, then that person's income plus $B$'s would exactly equal the sum of $A$'s and $C$'s. Such an operation would be inappropriate in the case of prestige. One cannot add the prestige of $A$ to that of $C$ in any meaningful sense. Whenever it is possible to compare differences in scores because of the existence of such a standardized unit, we refer to the scale as an *interval scale.*

If, in addition, there is a nonarbitrary zero point, it then becomes possible to compare the ratio of two scores, and we have what is termed a *ratio scale.* In practice, whenever we have a definite unit of measurement, such as the dollar or millimeter, we will in fact have a meaningful zero point (no income or no length). In these cases we may also compare ratios and make meaningful statements, such as that one person's income is twice that of another.[1]

Of course, the aim of all scientists is to improve measurement as much as possible and to utilize as many interval or ratio scales as is feasible, given the limitations of knowledge and cost. But it is often extremely difficult in the social sciences to obtain true interval or ratio scales. Ordinal scales are much more frequent. One of the most challenging tasks confronting social scientists is to improve measurement, and a number of rather ingenious though indirect procedures have been developed toward that end.

The major point we want to emphasize is that it is by no means a simple task even to conceptualize what our variables or scales should be. We must usually begin with relatively obvious manifest characteristics that yield nothing more than nominal scales and cross-classifications. Then when we find certain of these to be useful, in the sense of enabling us to predict to other variables or classifications, we must undertake the more difficult task of conceptualizing the variables that underlie or explain these simple relationships. At the same time, we must find practical ways of measuring them. We need to use the easily identifiable relationships, plus whatever intuitive insights we may have, to develop theories involving more abstract variables with greater explanatory power.

## THE INDIRECTNESS OF MEASUREMENT

Perhaps the most frequently encountered objection to efforts at precise measurement in the social sciences is that measurement is often highly indirect. It is true that all measurement is to some degree indirect, even in

1.  Perhaps the most familiar example of an interval scale that is not at the same time a ratio scale is temperature, as measured in terms of either Celsius or Fahrenheit degrees. Since the zero points on both of these scales are arbitrary, one does not say that 40° is twice as hot as 20°, though it *is* meaningful to compare this difference with the difference between, say, 80° and 60°.

physics, the most precise science with which the social sciences can be compared. But while social scientists can readily point to this fact and argue by analogy that their problems are basically no different from those of physical scientists, the difficulty is an important one. To illustrate its generality, while at the same time indicating some special difficulties facing the social scientist, we can begin by briefly considering a simple measurement problem in physics.

Even on the intuitive level, we have learned to think of the "mass" of a body in terms of some kind of postulated property or quality involving a quantity of matter. Yet the measurement of mass is not as direct as is sometimes supposed. Basically, the measurement of such quantities as mass (or temperature) involves obtaining the readings of a pointer on the dial of a measuring instrument under standardized conditions, and then inferring a body's mass on the basis of such pointer readings. A causal interpretation of the measurement process can be constructed somewhat as follows. The actual pointer reading one obtains from the instrument or scale is determined by a number of factors, only one of which is the presumed mass of the body. If a spring scale is being used, the pointer reading is determined by (1) the mass of the body, (2) the gravitational force of the earth, (3) properties of the scale itself (e.g., properties of the metal spring), (4) properties of the scientist who reads the scale, and (5) numerous miscellaneous factors, none of which has any major significance.

How, then, do we infer "mass" from the pointer reading? In effect, we do so by making more or less realistic assumptions about the other variables that could possibly affect the readings. Sometimes these assumptions can be made on the basis of theory or a well-established set of empirical "facts." In this example, the gravitational force of the earth is assumed to be known, and adjustments can be made for any elevation above sea level. We recognize a certain circularity in this kind of theoretical argument, since certain prior theoretical assumptions must have been made in order to find a starting point. In this example, it might reasonably be assumed that the effects of the earth's gravitational pull are constant, or unchanging, from one replication to the next, so that any differences in pointer readings could not be attributed to that particular factor. This illustrates the general observation that the existence of an adequate theory often assists the measurement process.

Continuing with the illustration, properties of the scale itself, such as the quality of the metal spring, might also account for the pointer readings. It is usually assumed that the measuring instrument possesses certain constant properties, and that it has been well calibrated by comparing its pointer readings with those of some other standardized scale. Again, the argument is a bit circular. How does one know that the properties of the standard scale are really constant? Perhaps all such scales have changing properties known only to a mysterious actor who manipulates these properties so that they all change in the same way. We simply assume that this is not the case and that the properties of the measuring instrument can be taken as constant over the period of observation. Therefore we must not only make theoretical assumptions, but we must make assumptions about our measuring instruments.

There are also the varying properties of the observer, and countless minor disturbances of intervening influences. Recognizing, for example, that any human observer's judgment regarding the coincidence of a pointer with a given line will depend on the condition of the observer's eyes and numerous psychological factors, the observer relies on mechanical or electronic substitutes insofar as possible. As a final caution, the observer insists on *repeated* measurements, or replication, in order to cancel out the effects of random disturbances. Ultimately, then, the observer can only make probability statements that depend upon the assumption that disturbances are operating in accordance with known laws of probability. If they are operating in some unknown systematic manner, the observer may obtain biased measures, and any inferences based on these measures may be faulty.

Exactly the same principles apply to measurement in the social sciences, but it is unfortunately much more difficult to make realistic assumptions about disturbances. This is due to a combination of reasons. First, we lack the well-grounded theories specifying other forces (e.g., gravity) that might be operating. Second, we cannot be so easily assured that our measuring instruments are well calibrated against an objective standard or that they possess constant properties. If we get different results from one replication to the next, we will have difficulty separating real changes from those resulting from the measurement process itself. Finally, there are a number of practical reasons why repeated measurements are both more difficult and less useful in the case of human subjects.

Therefore, while we may legitimately claim that the basic problems of measurement are similar from one science to the next, this simple assertion masks a number of real difficulties that the social scientist must face, since all measurement is necessarily indirect. "Indirectness" is a matter of degree, and in general the more indirect the measurement the larger the number of untested assumptions that must be strung together in order to make valid tests of one's theory.

In order to make this general point much more specific, the intriguing problem of attitude measurement can be used. Are there any rigorous ways of inferring what is going on inside a person's mind by examining the patterning of his or her responses to written tests? How and why is this problem more complex than that of inferring the properties of a body (e.g., its mass) on the basis of its behavior when placed on a scale? Are human beings so variable or so whimsical that the task is virtually hopeless? Are there ways of obtaining repeated measures without at the same time changing the person being studied?

### Attitude Measurement

Suppose an investigator wishes to test the hypothesis that the greater a person's political conservatism, the greater his or her general prejudice toward ethnic minorities. It will obviously be necessary to measure both prejudice and political conservatism, neither of which may have been very clearly defined in the theoretical explanation. Even if specific definitions are given for both concepts, it will still be necessary to cope with a number of important problems in constructing a set of questions designed to measure each variable.

One basic decision concerns the level of generality on which the hypothesis is to be tested. Is the prejudice directed toward *all* ethnic minorities or just one, such as Hispanics? And which Hispanic group? What areas of political conservatism are to be tapped? Economic conservatism? Conservatism with respect to civil liberties? Social welfare programs? International relations? And how specific should the items be? Should they refer to particular pieces of legislation currently before Congress? To particular actions taken by federal agencies? To policies being implemented by the Administration?

The basic dilemma is that specific questions are often necessary in order to make items relevant to respondents. They may have definite ideas regarding the government's role in foreign affairs, yet they may respond in the socially approved manner to a general question about the abstract rights of minorities or the right of individuals to a fair trial. If questions are made too specific, they immediately become dated and of little general interest. If someone wished to replicate the study five years later, some of the court decisions and legislative initiatives would have become dead issues. Nor could the study be replicated in other countries with any assurance that the same variables were being measured. A French citizen might disapprove of the intervention of the United States in the internal affairs of another country, while similarly endorsing increased integration of minorities within the United States. This, however, would tell us very little about that citizen's general level of prejudice or degree of political conservatism. One would have to find a set of items or measures relevant to French society.

Thus finding measurement instruments sensitive enough to distinguish among different levels of a variable, such as prejudice, may require the use of highly specific items. But this conflicts with the aim of developing measures that are sufficiently general to be applied to a wide variety of contexts and over a reasonable period of time. Even very general questions may have different meanings to various persons. A skeptic can always claim that the questions may be tapping a different underlying motive or attitude in different contexts. One answer to such a skeptic is to disclaim any intention of inferring anything beyond the actual responses to the questions. That is, we may say that we are not really interested in the underlying attitudes but merely in the responses themselves. This answer is obviously unsatisfactory. Why select a particular set of perhaps ten questions out of literally thousands that might be asked?

A second crucial decision concerns the degree to which the purposes of the measurement should be disguised. How do we know that the respondents will tell us how they really feel and think? Perhaps they will merely tell us what they think we want to hear or what they consider to be the socially approved answer. There seem to be two basic ways to resolve this kind of difficulty. The first is to make no effort to disguise the fact that the questions are designed to get at prejudice, conservatism, or some other controversial topic, but to assure the respondent that it is to his or her advantage to be perfectly candid.

If this approach is used, the interviewer must go to great lengths to achieve good rapport, assure respondents that they will remain anonymous, and guarantee that there is no possible way their answers can jeopardize them. In addition, an appeal can be made that respondents are representing other people like themselves, which is quite true, and that the investigator needs to know what they really think. Once such rapport and trust have been established, most respondents are willing to talk freely about very controversial subjects, and the researcher may then assume that no systematic biases have been introduced. In a few instances, it is possible to build in cross-checks by asking essentially the same question in several different ways; but a clever respondent can fool the investigator in numerous imaginative ways if he or she so desires. The critical objective is to persuade the individual that there is no reason to be that creative!

But perhaps respondents are only fooling themselves. The above strategy presupposes that the respondent is a rational individual who is conscious of his or her true attitudes and who also has a definite opinion about most of the questions being asked. What if these assumptions are false? Or what if the respondents recognize their prejudice but guard it carefully against all intruders, even the most friendly and reassuring interviewer? Or what if the subject is so controversial that very few respondents can be expected to cooperate?

A second general strategy can then be used. This approach depends on the assumption that if the true purpose of the study can be carefully disguised, respondents' underlying motives and attitudes can be inferred through the skillful analysis of their responses to very vague stimuli that elicit open-ended answers. For example, the person interviewed may be shown a set of pictures, some of which involve both minorities and nonminorities, and may be asked to construct a story about each of them. Prejudice is then inferred from a study of the written stories. Or conservatism might be inferred from responses to a set of items that do not directly refer to social issues but to hypothetical relations with parents, children, or religious authorities.

These *projective techniques*—that is, techniques that permit individuals' more genuine attitudes to be "projected onto" other objects, events, or issues—are not without their own problems. Measurement becomes much more indirect and open to diverse interpretation. The biases of the investigator may very well intrude. One person reading the stories, for example, may perceive a large amount of disguised hostility toward minorities whereas a second person may not. The interpretations of the stories may tell much more about the researcher than about the respondent. In order to avoid this complication, social scientists who use such projective techniques have developed rather elaborate standardized ways of scoring the information obtained. However, only with well-trained scorers can a high level of agreement on how to score each respondent be achieved, and there is always a question remaining about how much disagreement would prevail among scorers trained in very different settings.

There are many points at which an unreasonable critic may fault *any* study, no matter how carefully designed and carried out, but this is especially the case where attitude measurement is concerned. The task of the researcher is therefore to convince the reasonable skeptic that a large number of precautions have been taken and that others might have been taken had it not been for limitations of time, money, setting, or existing knowledge.

## INFERRING DIMENSIONALITY

One of the most challenging problems confronting the student of attitude measurement is that of ***dimensionality.*** Dimensionality refers to how one tells whether the questions being used are measuring a single basic attitude or several different attitudes at the same time. Are several diverse dimensions being tapped, or is it realistic to assume that individuals can be ranked along a single continuum from high to low, favorable to unfavorable, or liberal to conservative?

It has been historically true that in most cases where investigators have studied what they thought to be a single dimension— say, prejudice or political conservatism—they have later inferred that two or more distinct dimensions were involved. This discovery may result in a considerable refinement of common sense. For example, both prejudice and political conservatism clearly have multiple distinct dimensions. Persons who are liberal with respect to one set of issues may or may not be liberal with respect to others. Therefore the simple distinction between "liberals" and "conservatives," or "radicals" and "reactionaries," may be highly misleading both practically and theoretically. The same point can be applied to many other phenomena— for example, parenting behavior, mental illness, or attitudes toward deviant behavior.

The use of simple scoring procedures may prevent us from realizing that a given set of questions is tapping more than one attitude dimension. The questions may force a particular ordering on the data, so that individuals are automatically ranked from high to low regardless of the resulting patterns of responses. This is often found in very common attitude scales that are constructed by merely adding the scores for each separate question.

Suppose respondents have been given a set of items and are asked to indicate whether they "strongly agree," "agree," "are neutral or have no opinion," "disagree," or "strongly disagree." Scores may then be assigned to their responses by some arbitrary system (say, scoring the above responses as 5,4,3,2, and 1 respectively). This is done for each of the questions and a total score obtained. Some of the questions will be worded oppositely, so that on one item an "agree" answer indicates a high degree of, say, prejudice, whereas a "disagree" indicates a high degree of that attitude on the next item; but this can more easily be handled by reversing the scores on (for example) the second item.

To illustrate, two statements might be:

1.  Blacks and whites should live in different neighborhoods.
2.  Blacks should be given exactly the same political rights as whites.

Scores might be constructed so that high scores indicate high prejudice. In the above example, a person who "strongly agrees" with the first statement and "disagrees" with the second might receive a score of 5 on the first question and 4 on the second; someone who "disagrees" with the first and who is neutral on the second would receive scores of 2 and 3 on the respective items.

Since everyone will receive some numerical total score, simply adding the scores will automatically rank all individuals regardless of what items happened to be used. In fact, one could readily construct a nonsense "scale" consisting, let us say, of ten disconnected questions. In such a case, most people's scores would come out somewhere near the middle of the possible range, but just by chance some might receive scores near the maximum or minimum. They could then be ranked along the "dimension" concerned. It is in this sense that we can say that the method forces an ordering on the data. If all the items actually measure a single attitudinal dimension, then all is well. But if they do not, the result is likely to be a nonsense conclusion, if it could be recognized as such, or—much worse—a misleading conclusion.

### Factor Analysis

One obvious solution to the dimensionality problem is to study the individual questions to see whether they fit together properly. Presumably, if they are all measuring the same thing, then the items ought to be correlated with each other. For instance, if our intention is to study attitudes toward having children, all the questions used should measure those attitudes, and answers to one question should be highly related to answers to the others. But we cannot expect perfect relationships, since each question will have its idiosyncratic aspects for any given individual. A person who is generally negative about children may have had some pleasant contacts with them that lead him or her to accept having children under certain circumstances. A second person may have strong opinions about parenting because of experiences in his or her own family. Because each question has its personal aspects, which can be thought of as producing chance or random measurement error, it is usually desirable to use at least five or six items. This is actually one of the social scientist's forms of replication. In studying how well the questions fit together, the social scientist is trying to determine the degree to which replications involve measures of the same thing.

In general, the less directly related the questions are to the specific attitude being studied, the less highly correlated we would expect them to be with each other, and the more opportunity arises for random interference, or "noise." But this is not necessarily the case, since a number of items might be measuring some other attitudinal dimension not explicitly taken into consideration. It therefore becomes necessary to study the *patterns* of intercorrelations among items, as well as their absolute magnitudes.

But as soon as we admit this kind of difficulty, simple common-sense methods are inappropriate. To illustrate, suppose an investigator measures attitudes toward government regulation using twelve questions, four of which tap attitudes toward government regulation in business and industry, four with respect to civil liberties, and four regarding social welfare programs. Let us assume that in reality each of these three dimensions of attitudes toward regulation are completely unrelated to each other. That is, if we knew that a person were against government regulation with respect to economic issues, this would tell us absolutely nothing about his or her attitudes concerning regulation in the civil liberties area or with respect to social programs. In this case, people who are against regulation on economic issues are no more or less likely to be against regulation with respect to civil liberties than are those who are for regulation on economic issues.

This situation could be diagrammed as in Figure 3–1, in which the three

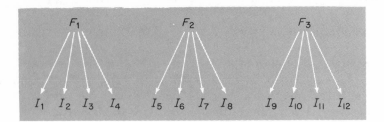

**Figure 3-1**  Simple Factor Analysis Model Involving Three Uncorrelated Factors and Indicators, Each Linked to Only One Factor.

distinct dimensions of attitudes toward regulation have been designated as $F_1$, $F_2$, and $F_3$, and where the issues or items have been designated as $I_1$, $I_2, \ldots, I_{12}$. The underlying attitudinal dimensions represented by the $F$'s are referred to as "factors" and the responses to the twelve questions as "indicators" or measures of these factors.

In the diagram of Figure 3-1, items 1 to 4 are indicators of $F_1$, which we are taking to be antiregulation attitudes on economic issues; items 5 to 8 are indicators of $F_2$, civil liberties; and items 9 to 12 are indicators of $F_3$, social welfare programs. The lack of arrows connecting the $F$'s represents the fact that we are for the time being assuming that these factors are completely uncorrelated. The basic assumption behind this kind of model is that the underlying attitudes or mental states actually cause the individual to respond in given ways to the twelve items. Of course other factors will also affect each response, but we assume that whatever these may be, they do not affect the *patterning* of responses. Put another way, we may conceive of the responses to each question as having been caused by one of the three factors, plus a number of variables that are uniquely related to that single item.

If these assumptions are in fact correct, we would anticipate that items 1 to 4 would be intercorrelated with each other due to the common influence of $F_1$. We consider them to be spuriously related due to their common cause (in this instance, antiregulation attitudes on economic issues). If $F_1$ could be directly measured and controlled, the intercorrelations among these four items should reduce to zero, since their remaining causes would have nothing in common. The same should apply to the item sets 5 to 8 and 9 to 12.

But if we were to examine the relationships *between* item sets, we would expect to find all intercorrelations to be approximately zero. That is, item 1 should not be related to items 5 to 12, and so forth. Knowing how a person responded to a question dealing with regulation of the economy (say, endorsement of wage-and-price controls) should not help us whatsoever in predicting how that person will respond to any of the civil liberties or the social welfare questions. Thus in this simple situation, we would expect to find three sets of four indicators each, with correlations *within* sets being reasonably high but with very low correlations *between* sets. If such simple results were actually found, we might infer that the twelve questions were tapping three unrelated factors; and by looking carefully at the wording of the questions in each set, we might infer the underlying factors.

Unfortunately, we seldom get such simple, and clear-cut results. It is much more likely that some interrelationships among items will be strong, others will be moderate, and still others approximately zero. Adequate measures of the strength of these interrelationships plus a much more rigorous procedure for inferring the underlying factors will be required. Such measures and procedures exist, but the subject is far too technical to be discussed in the present context.

However, two complications that may arise will suggest the kinds of ap-

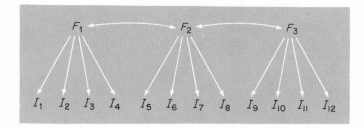

**Figure 3-2** Factor Analysis Model Involving Correlated Factors.

proaches that can be used. One of these possibilities is diagrammed in Figure 3-2 and the second in Figure 3-3. Obviously the two situations can be combined, and it is possible that many more than three factors will be operating. In Figure 3-2, the three factors are themselves interrelated, as indicated by the curved arrows connecting them.

For example, we would ordinarily predict that people who favor regulation of the economy also favor regulation to protect civil liberties and to ensure that the resources of social welfare programs go to those most legitimately in need of them. If so, and the assumptions we have made seem reasonable, then we would expect to find correlations or associations among all pairs of questions, although in most cases the correlations within any given set should be stronger than those between sets. That is, item 1 should be more highly related to, or predictive of, items 2 to 4 than to the remaining items. If this kind of pattern prevails consistently, then we might infer that the model of Figure 3-2 is the correct one.

But it is also possible that a single item will measure more than one factor, as illustrated in Figure 3-3. A question may be double-barreled, measuring both civil liberties and social welfare. Suppose item 4 tapped both $F_1$ and $F_2$. Then this particular item should be correlated with sets 1 to 3 and 5 to 8, though perhaps it might be less highly related to any of them than would be expected if it clearly belonged to one set or the other.

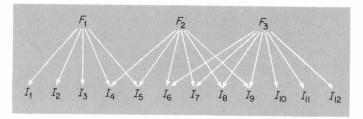

**Figure 3-3** Factor Analysis Model Involving Multiple Links between Factors and Indicators.

In more complex examples, a simple inspection of the correlations among items will not be sufficient to enable us to infer the underlying factors. What is needed are quantitative techniques that make it possible to estimate the degree to which each item is measuring each factor, as well as the number of such factors and their interrelationships. It turns out that although such techniques exist and have been well studied under the label of *factor analysis,* there are too many unknowns in the theoretical system to give unique estimates of the factors without further assumptions.

It again becomes necessary to supplement the empirical analysis with theoretical assumptions, many of which will be inherently untestable and some of which will be more plausible than others. Once more, the hyper-critical skeptic can always question these assumptions. The careful social scientist will always caution the consumer of research that these assumptions are being made, so that the more reasonable skeptic can make constructive suggestions for improving the research.

### Guttman Scaling

We should consider one other kind of procedure for inferring dimensionality. This is particularly useful where the objective is to reduce the number of items to a relatively small number that measure a single dimension. This procedure is referred to as *Guttman scaling* and is based on a very simple principle and definition of a cumulative (ordinal) scale. The basic idea is that if individuals can be properly ranked along a single continuum or dimension, producing an ordinal scale, then if *A* is greater than *B,* he or she should possess all of the attributes of *B* plus at least one more. In terms of attitudinal questions, if *A* is more conservative than *B,* then that individual should endorse all of the conservative items that *B* has endorsed plus at least one more.

This principle can be illustrated in terms of an arithmetic test consisting of items that get more and more difficult. Suppose there are five such items. Presumably a person who misses only one question should solve the first four easier questions and miss the last. Someone who misses two questions should solve the first three correctly and miss the last two. If this pattern prevails perfectly, then it will be possible to tell exactly which questions a person missed if we know his or her total score. This criterion, of course, does not allow for careless mistakes, or "errors." No one is supposed to miss the first question and get the others correct.

Using the variable prejudice again, it has been found empirically that what sociologists call "social distance" items often form this kind of cumulative scale with very few "errors." At the one extreme can be placed an item involving a personal commitment to racial intermarriage, such as "Would you be willing to marry a black person?" Somewhat less extreme would be a question tapping one's willingness to associate intimately with blacks as social equals, such as "Would you be willing to have a black person in your home as an overnight guest?''At the opposite extreme would be a question such as ''Would you be willing to shop at a store where there are black customers?'' Presumably any white who is willing to marry a black person would be willing to have a black as an overnight guest, and a white who would be willing to have the black person as a guest would be willing to shop near one. But a white person who is willing to have a black overnight guest may not be willing to marry a black.

If the five items formed a perfect scale, then they could be arranged in order according to degree of favorableness implied. If each item involved a yes-no response (to simplify the example), the results might be as shown in Table 3–2.

In a perfect scale, there will be a diagonal pattern of $X$'s and exactly one more type of response pattern than there are questions (with yes-no answers). In this example there are two persons who answered ''yes'' to all five questions. Three answered ''no'' to the first question (say, dealing with marriage) but ''yes'' to all of the remaining four questions. Two persons failed to endorse the first two questions but answered ''yes'' to the remaining three, and so forth. Notice that there are no peculiar or idiosyncratic answers, such as that of answering ''no'' only to the fourth question. Of course, with real data we will never obtain such clear-cut results. There will always be ''errors,'' which will show up as $X$'s in peculiar, off-diagonal locations.

The problem is how to deal with such ''errors.'' If there are very few

Table 3–2    Response Pattern Representing a Perfect Guttman Scale

| PERSONS | ITEMS | | | | | | | | | |
|---|---|---|---|---|---|---|---|---|---|---|
| | 1 Yes | 2 Yes | 3 Yes | 4 Yes | 5 Yes | 1 No | 2 No | 3 No | 4 No | 5 No |
| Type 1 | X | X | X | X | X | | | | | |
| | X | X | X | X | X | | | | | |
| Type 2 | | X | X | X | X | X | | | | |
| | | X | X | X | X | X | | | | |
| | | X | X | X | X | X | | | | |
| Type 3 | | | X | X | X | X | X | | | |
| | | | X | X | X | X | X | | | |
| Type 4 | | | | X | X | X | X | X | | |
| Type 5 | | | | | X | X | X | X | X | |
| | | | | | X | X | X | X | X | |
| Type 6 | | | | | | X | X | X | X | X |
| | | | | | | X | X | X | X | X |

off-diagonal $X$'s, and if they appear to be randomly scattered, then they can perhaps be considered as true errors, or as idiosyncratic responses due to peculiar experiences of the respondents. But what if there were as many as 20 percent "errors"? And suppose most of these involved interchanges between questions 2 and 3. How do we know they are true errors? In fact, we would probably feel rather foolish if we were to confront white respondents and tell them they had been "in error" (or inconsistent) if they had indicated a willingness to have a black supervisor, but not a black neighbor. Just because most whites might be more willing to have a black neighbor than a black supervisor, does this mean that these particular respondents are in some sense in error or irrational?

This problem seems to reduce to whether or not the investigator wishes to *assume* that there is a single underlying dimension and that departures from a perfect scale are to be considered as response errors, or whether he or she is willing to admit a greater degree of complexity. For example, it is entirely possible that the items are tapping two distinct dimensions and that items 2 and 3 stand in different relationships to each other on these two dimensions. If item 2 represents a higher degree of prejudice on the first dimension, but item 3 represents a higher degree on the second, then some individuals will answer "yes" to question 2 and "no" to question 3, whereas others will reverse the pattern.

The existence of large numbers of *patterned* errors therefore suggests the possibility that more than one dimension is being measured. Again it becomes necessary to develop reasonably technical criteria for deciding which alternative explanation to accept, and once more the skeptic may choose whichever explanation the investigator rejects. It is therefore essential that both be well aware of the criteria that are being used, as well as the mathematical properties of the scaling procedures.

The field of attitude measurement illustrates very well many of the problems and possibilities of indirect measurement and dimensionality. However, it should be pointed out that techniques such as factor analysis and Guttman scaling can be applied in a number of areas in addition to attitude measurement. Nevertheless, this brief discussion of attitude measurement indicates some of the complexities and the necessity for careful quantitative work. A great deal has already been accomplished, even though much more needs to be done. While it is essential that investigators resolve these issues, the process through which one responds to this challenge is rewarding and exciting, since attitudes are an intriguing area of research.

## MEASUREMENT OF GROUP PROPERTIES

Social scientists face many other kinds of measurement problems, only some of which can be discussed in an overview such as this. While many psychologists deal almost exclusively with generalizations about individuals (animals as well as human beings), other social scientists are more concerned with propositions about groups of one kind or another. These range from small cliques, families, and communities to entire societies. Nevertheless, much of our data are available in the form of measures on individuals or small groups, which raises the problem of developing ways of aggregating, or summarizing, these individual measures so as to construct measures that are appropriate to the entire group.

There have been numerous philosophical debates over the question of whether persons are more "real" than groups, and whether group characteristics are a reflection of individual attributes. One extreme position is that groups are simply aggregates of individuals, that they possess a "reality" only in the minds of social scientists, and that there is little to be gained from studying them as distinct entities. Another position, by contrast, stresses that groups have existences quite apart from those of their individual members, though of course they remain intangible and would cease to exist if all of their members were to disappear. Much of this debate turns on ambiguous questions concerning what one means by the statement that groups "exist." There is no need to enter into such a debate here except to point out that, quite apart from questions of the reality of groups, it is often *useful* to make statements about groups and to measure group properties that are very different from those of single individuals.

A few examples should clarify this point. Political scientists speak about the behavior of nations, and they analyze competition among nations in much the same way as a psychologist might analyze competition among siblings. It is useful to classify nations or societies in terms of size, forms of government, homogeneity with respect to various characteristics, religious systems, gross national products, and so forth. One may then state theoretical propositions relating size to concentration of political power, the nature of economic systems to political systems, and so forth, and data may be collected and analyzed in much the same way as is done in the case of persons. The number of "cases" becomes the number of nations, but otherwise the basic principles and strategies of analysis are the same. But the practical measurement problems are in many respects more difficult.

Foremost among these practical problems is that data collection involves great expenditures of time and money. It is expensive enough to conduct a careful survey of two thousand persons in a single city. But if comparable data were to be collected on persons in as many as two hundred cities, the cost would be prohibitive. A great deal of social research is conducted by single individuals or small research teams with very limited budgets, and therefore comparative work on large numbers of large-scale units such as communities or societies is practically always confined to what are referred to as "secondary analyses" of data that have been collected for other purposes. In some cases, these data are excellent and well standardized from one community to another. Such is the case with respect to the U.S. Census and other censuses in modern Westernized societies. Censuses conducted in less industrialized countries, however, have tended to be incomplete and often biased in unknown ways.

Whenever the social scientist wishes to deal with groups as large as entire societies, it becomes extremely difficult to obtain truly comparable data. Even where there are high-quality data in each nation, the definitions used in collecting and classifying these data are often very different from one country to the next. In one country the definition of an "urban" area may be any community of five thousand or more population; in a second it may be one of ten thousand or more; and in a third it may be two thousand. Countries are divided into very different types of units (e.g., states, cantons, provinces), each of which may have its own policies with respect to the collection of data. Even within a single country, policies of local units may vary considerably. For example, crime statistics in the United States are notoriously poor and underestimate actual crime rates by unknown degrees. Some kinds of crimes, such as homicides, are much more likely to come to the attention of authorities than are others, such as rape; and official crime rates are very likely to reflect differential reporting by the public and differential law enforcement practices by police.

Whenever social scientists are forced to use secondary sources of data, they almost always must settle for measures other than those they would prefer to obtain. In many instances the information is not available because the collecting agency had a policy against gathering it, or it never occurred to them to collect it, or there was no pressure applied by special interest groups to collect it. Obviously, a census is a very expensive operation, as is a public opinion poll, and only a small fraction of the potentially useful questions can be asked. And, of course, a given respondent cannot be asked too many questions, since a threshold of approximately one hour of interviewing time has generally been found optimal in keeping refusal rates at a reasonable level.

This difficulty with individual respondents raises a second major problem of measurement in studying larger units, one which has yet to receive the careful attention of most social scientists, except possibly economists. Many of the measures or variables appropriate to groups must be obtained by aggregating scores for persons. One simple aggregate measure is the size of the group, obtained by simply counting all its members. There are many other kinds of aggregate measures that can be similarly obtained—namely, those that involve percentages of the members who belong in various categories. Cities or counties can be characterized by variables such as percent black, percent of the labor force that is unemployed or white collar, or by measures of what is typical, such as median income, mean years of schooling, or average age of dwelling units. More complex derived measures can also be constructed. For example, by counting the relative numbers of whites and non-whites in all city blocks, a measure of residential segregation can be computed for each city.

Much more difficult problems of aggregation arise when it is clear that not all persons should receive the same weights, but no exact weighting criteria can be easily developed. Suppose one wanted to obtain a measure of the average attitudinal "climate" toward gun control in each of one hundred communities. Obviously some people should be given more weight than others, since they will not all be equally influential. But how does one decide how much weight to give the mayor, the newspaper editor, or leaders of pro- and antigun control organizations? One would need an accurate measure of influence, which would be extremely expensive to obtain. Furthermore, the weights assigned to each individual would have to differ according to each issue area being studied. Someone with considerable impact on attitudes toward the use of handguns might have very little influence on some other related issue. And unless at least an interval-scale level of measurement can be attained for the measures of individual attitudes, their separate scores cannot be legitimately "added" or averaged. Many of these subtle problems of forming aggregate measures have not yet been well studied, since few social scientists have had the necessary resources to collect adequate data in the first place. But sooner or later they must be resolved if measurement is to be improved.

A third difficulty stems from the fact that groups often have vague or arbitrary boundaries that have been drawn for political, organizational, or other practical reasons. There can be no doubt where John Jones ends and Bill Brown begins, and therefore persons may be counted and sorted into mutually exclusive and exhaustive categories. But exactly what are the boundaries of the urban sprawl of Los Angeles? What are the boundaries of small groups? Most informal cliques have members that come and go. Although churches and other voluntary organizations may have membership lists, many persons so listed are not really members in any sociological sense. And many individuals identify with the goals of organizations to which they do not pay dues. Many groups have memberships that overlap imperceptibly. Those responsible for constructing membership lists are well aware of the ambiguities involved. Organizers may engage in endless discussions about whether a particular individual is really an integral part of a certain group. This routine activity reflects the same kind of problem with which social scientists must learn to deal rigorously in the research process.

The problem of indistinct group boundaries has been especially troublesome to anthropologists studying so-called "primitive" peoples. Unlike the nation-state, a primitive society may be very loosely defined. Is it a single community? Or several communities bound together by political ties? Or a clustering of communities linked by a common language or economy? Different investigators may reach different conclusions depending on the criteria they prefer. This research problem does not exist as long as one's attention is confined to persons or to readily distinguishable units of any kind.

Closely related to the problem of group boundaries is the problem of mutual influence across ill-defined boundaries. Suppose, for example, that a group of anthropologists wants to study the influence of economic systems on political development. One investigator may choose to divide Africa into one hundred societies, whereas a second might distinguish only twenty-nine. Obviously the first investigator is using smaller units, which provide more cases for statistical purposes. But suppose many of these societies are so closely interconnected that they merely borrow ideas from each other, as of course occurs with other kinds of social groupings as well. Both anthropologists may be theoretically interested in the causal processes that produce a practical connection between economic and political systems. They would be on solid ground if they could assume that each society constituted an independent replication, in the same sense that each flip of a coin is statistically independent of the others or each replication of an experiment is independent of all others.[2]

The problem with adjacent societies, however, and with adjacent groups of people, is that they tend to influence each other in ways that may distort inferences about the true causal processes. If one society has a complex division of labor and political system, and if its neighbor appears to be very similar, it is difficult to tell to what degree each developed autonomously and to what degree they should really be treated as one and the same society. This particular problem can only be analyzed by complex statistical procedures. It closely parallels problems faced by economists who take repeated measures of the same units (such as business firms) over many points in time. Factors affecting the outcomes at time 1 may be highly related to factors affecting them at times 2 and 3, again a case in which repeated observations are not independent.

It is usually found that the smaller the time intervals, and the smaller the group units, the more serious the difficulty. This limits the number of pieces into which the pie can be sliced. If a social scientist really believed that the size of one unit was as good as that of another, he or she would simply use a very large number of small units (e.g., counties instead of states), thereby either increasing the size of the sample or cutting down the amount of work. But as usual, life is never that simple. At each decision point there will be pros and cons to consider, and it is often unfortunately true that such decisions must be made on the basis of enlightened guesses rather than solid facts. But as a science matures, the relative proportion of guesses is progressively reduced.

The need to maintain the linkages between theory and measurement should now be clearer. The same scientific connections must be sustained between measurement and design. The research design provides a framework within which research activity is carried on, a plan for controlling certain

---

2.    The idea of statistical independence can be pinned down by saying that if two events are independent, then knowing the outcome of one does not help us predict the outcome of the other. Knowing that an honest coin has come up heads on the first flip does not help us predict what will happen on the next flip.

variables (keeping them unchanged) while manipulating (changing) others. It seeks to guarantee that the effects of the latter changes can be separated out from other factors, and the qualities of those effects identified. Imposing such a framework is necessary if the investigator is to be able to test whether or not the explanation proposed is supported by the information eventually collected.

# CHAPTER 4
# RESEARCH DESIGN

*In formal logic, a contradiction is the signal of a defeat; but in the evolution of real knowledge it marks the first step in progress towards a victory.*

Research designs, and methods of data collection and analysis, are essential to the research process. However, if the researcher lacks a well-conceived theoretical explanation, and adequate operationally defined measures of the key variables in that explanation, the most sophisticated research designs and methods will to varying degrees represent wasted effort. The results of the research will be difficult to relate to other empirical findings, and to generalize to other similar phenomena. They may be too narrow, too unreliable, or too lacking in validity to be useful in explaining the problem of interest. But if the theoretical and measurement prerequisites have been satisfactorily met, the application of an appropriate design and set of methods greatly enhances the value and utility of the research. A poor design and inappropriate methods of data collection and analysis will negate the advantages of a good theoretical model and broad, clearly defined measures. In building a knowledge base that integrates information about a number of related phenomena, equal attention and competence must be directed to all these aspects of research.

Therefore, this and the following chapter will explain some basic ideas about research design and briefly outline some methods used in the social sciences for collecting and analyzing data within such designs. What is commonly meant by *design* is a general set of operating guidelines within which research is carried out consistent with the scientific method. Data collection and analysis *methods* refer to specific research strategies for gathering and analyzing information relevant to the particular explanation being tested or explored.

If we were to explore, for example, the relationship between public attitudes toward comprehensive national health care, as the major dependent variable, and several independent variables such as sex, age, education, occupation, and family size, we would want to construct the kind of research design and use the kind of data collection and analytic methods most likely to yield the most accurate explanation of the relationships proposed, given the environmental constraints placed on the research.

A research design is in this sense an application of scientific method to the particular problem to be investigated, a phenomenon about which the researcher or theorist seeks greater insights and an increased body of factual knowledge. As the intent of the scientific method is to provide general guidelines for *abstracting* and *generalizing* ideas about specific phenomena, appropriate research designs and methods contain explicit prescriptions for achieving that end. In reporting and assessing a piece of research, the *methodology,* or design and methods, of a study is a critical factor in judging the quality of the research. In this chapter we will focus on design issues.

## SOME PRINCIPLES
## OF EXPERIMENTAL DESIGN

The most rigorous and demanding design, one that makes optimal use of the scientific method and therefore provides the most accurate and valid information in testing explanations and theories, is the *experimental design.* It consists of a framework, or set of steps, within which attributes of selected variables can be *manipulated* (changed in value or degree), and their effect inferred under conditions that *control for* (or reduce) the influence of other variables that might also explain this effect. Such a framework permits the investigator to sort out the probable cause-and-effect relationships between the variables under study. In this sense, an experimental design is often treated as the most prestigious design within which to do research because it provides the most definitive, valid, and replicable facts, inferences, and insights.

However, many phenomena in the natural world, and many more in the socio-cultural world, do not lend themselves easily to the use of an experimental design. Ironically, it may be operationally impossible to apply an experimental design in studying "experimental social programs," because it is not possible to manipulate some of the significant variables under conditions that permit the control of other influential variables. For example, in studying the relationship between degree of work effort and the provision of "experimental" minimum income guarantees, it may not be possible to vary work-supportive variables such as extent of vocational training or child care while holding age, sex, education, and marital status constant. Therefore it may be impossible to study the effect of income benefits on number of hours worked within an ideal experimental design.

Furthermore, it is misguided to over-idealize experimental designs (which are most compatible with a laboratory setting) in studying complex events and issues when a diverse range of research designs can produce significant inferences and empirical knowledge. Nevertheless, all research efforts should approach the experimental design ideal as closely as feasible, realistic, and appropriate. Therefore, it is extremely important to understand its main premises and characteristics.

Experimental design is a complex subject that cannot be fully understood without a considerable background in statistics. That, however, should not deter us here. Since our main objective is to communicate and not overwhelm, we shall discuss only nontechnical issues. Let us begin with a very simple model of the ideal experiment. We will assume there are one or more important variables whose behaviors we wish to understand. We will refer to these as the *dependent* variables. We will further assume that the values of these variables are influenced by another set of variables that are possible causes of these dependent variables. These "causally-prior" variables are referred to as the *independent* variables. In addition, we will assume there are one or more variables whose effects we wish to control, or hold constant. By controlling, or *holding a variable constant,* we mean reducing a variable's influence to zero relative to the effects of the main variables to be studied. Those variables viewed by the researcher as advantageous to control within one study may be the main variables of interest in a subsequent study. In both cases, however, they represent the independent variables because we are assuming they have a prior causal effect.

For example, what if we are primarily interested in the relationship between physicians' attitudes toward male and female patients, and these physicians' typical patterns of prescribing treatment to these two groups? We would certainly learn a great deal more about this relationship if we could eliminate the influence, say, of private versus public health care settings—i.e., if we could hold health care setting constant for both groups of patients. In a subsequent study, however, we might be primarily interested in the relationship between setting and treatment methods, in which case we might want to control for physicians' attitudes. In both cases, physicians' attitudes and health care settings are independent variables, according to our assumptions, and treatment choices is the dependent variable.

In the ideal experiment, we need to isolate and infer the effects of one or more independent variables on the dependent variables. To simplify, we can assume for the time being that we are dealing with a single dependent variable, and that we wish to infer the effects of a single independent variable. To illustrate, let us suppose that occupational prestige is the dependent variable, and education the independent variable. Common sense would suggest that if it were possible to hold constant all of the remaining causes of the dependent

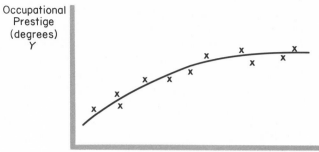

**Figure 4-1**  Hypothetical Data Representing a Nonlinear Relationship and a Close Fit between Education and Occupational Prestige.

variable, and if we could then systematically vary the single remaining independent variable (observing what happens to the dependent variable), we should then be able to infer the effects of the independent variable $X$ (level of education) on the dependent variable $Y$ (degree of occupational prestige). In particular, for each level of $X$, we ought to be able to associate some level of $Y$, as indicated in Figure 4-1.

Several things can be observed in Figure 4-1. First, not all the points fit exactly on a smooth curve. In the ideal, if all disturbing (additional explanatory) factors had been held constant, we might expect that all points would lie exactly on the curve. It is reasonable to ask, though, why the points are any more likely to fall on a smooth curve than on an irregular one, or why reality should conform to our simplest conceptions. Reality, in fact, may not oblige. But it is certainly convenient to believe that it does, because we can then describe the relationship through a simple mathematical formula and pretend that the deviations are either trivial or due to measurement errors. Oversimplifying reality is a necessity if we are to economize our thought processes and become more selective. This method is not peculiar to the social sciences. It holds true for all abstraction and generalization and has been used most systematically in the physical sciences.

The second thing to notice about Figure 4-1 is that the curve relating $X$ to $Y$ is not necessarily a straight line. The slope of the relationship between the variables changes. In this particular case, as $X$ increases $Y$ increases but at a decreasing rate. For example, at high levels of education a given increase in $X$ does not produce a very great change in the degree of occupational prestige $Y$—i.e., not nearly as large a change in $Y$ as when $X$ is small. The main point is that a mathematical curve is much more precise than the simple statement,"The greater the amount of one's education, the greater the occupational prestige of one's job." The experimenter may have begun with a crude verbal hypothesis of this sort, but the experimental result should not only seek to confirm the researcher's intuition but refine it, qualify it, and demonstrate the intricacies of the relationship.

Unfortunately, there is an extremely important assumption, so far ignored, for this shaped curve. That assumption assures us that all remaining causes of occupational prestige are controlled. But clearly there can be no well-conceived way of testing the assumption that they have been, since a skeptic can always think of some uncontrolled variable that might be a potential cause. Since it is impossible to list all possible causes and influences that might alter a relationship, it is also not possible to test this assumption.

Philosophers have written about this dilemma for centuries, and the notions of cause and effect have been perennially labeled problematic. This has not, fortunately for science, prevented research practitioners from using these concepts or their equivalents in the pursuit of knowledge, nor has it deterred them from conducting experiments and making inferences on the basis of their results. It has simply made them more cautious and humble, and has led them to make much more explicit the qualifications that accompany their research findings.

### Randomization and Systematic Controls

If we acknowledge honestly that this is a problem in applying scientific method, how can we resolve it? One thing to note is the following common result of experimentation: if the numerous disturbing (influencing) factors do *not* all act in concert, then we will usually find a distribution of results something like that in Figure 4–2, where the scores are scattered fairly widely about the smooth curve that has been drawn through them. That is, there is a relationship between *X* and *Y,* but the exact nature of that relationship is ambiguous. If there is a wide scattering of points, it will be much more difficult

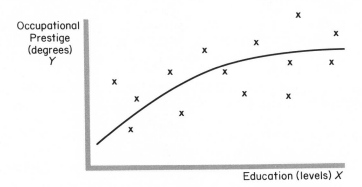

**Figure 4-2** Hypothetical Data Representing a Nonlinear Relationship and a Poor Fit between Education and Occupational Prestige.

to approximate them with any single smooth curve, and numerous curves will succeed almost equally well in fitting the data. Some criterion of what is meant by a "best fit" will then be necessary, and curve-fitting by simple inspection will have to be replaced by more rigorous methods that can be replicated by all observers.

The issue of *scatter* deserves further explanation. In discussing the correlation coefficient *r* in the theory chapter, we noted that *r* is a measure of *degree of association* that takes on the value of 1.0 whenever there is a perfect linear or straight-line relationship between two variables $X$ and $Y$. This will occur when all data points fall exactly on the line. Values of *r* that are less than 1.0 in numerical value may be interpreted as measuring the degree of *scatter* about the line. If points are randomly scattered, there will be no relationship between $X$ and $Y$, and *r* will take on a value of zero. In general, the greater the scatter the closer *r* will be to zero. In situations where the relationship between $X$ and $Y$ is not linear, as in Figure 4–2, we may devise similar measures of the "goodness of fit" of any specific mathematical curve to the data.[1]

With a substantial amount of scatter, there is always the strong chance that one or two uncontrolled variables are distorting the relationship between $X$ and $Y$. Perhaps there really is no causal relationship between level of education $X$ and degree of occupational prestige $Y$. As noted in Chapter 2, it is possible that a third variable $Z$ is a common cause of both $X$ and $Y$. If this is so, and $Z$ is not controlled, there might appear to be a causal relationship between them when in reality there is none. In such a case, we have referred to the relationship between $X$ and $Y$ as spurious. That is, it appears to be there in the data, but it is incorrect to infer from these data that educational level accounts for occupational prestige. The variables $X$ and $Y$ can only be said to be associated or *correlated*. We could in fact predict or estimate the one from the other. But there is no causal connection of practical or theoretical significance.

The problem is that the researcher may not be aware of the existence of $Z$ and its potential influence on $Y$. The greater the scatter of points, the more likely the presence of other disturbing explanatory influences. But the absence of scatter does not disprove the presence of other factors. Even with a perfect fit of the data to the curve, it is always possible that, had some third factor been held constant, the original relationship might have been significantly changed.

We have identified two kinds of "error" in this example: *truly random scatter* and *systematic distortions* produced by uncontrolled variables such as $Z$. In most research there are some errors of each type. Unfortunately the

---

1.    By convention, we construct these measures in such a way that they take on the upper limit of 1.0 whenever there is a perfect fit and become zero whenever there is a random scatter.

researcher is often not in a position to evaluate their relative magnitudes. The best resolution of the problem is to eliminate possible sources of error through the use of a careful research design. The question is how to accomplish this goal in the presence of very large numbers of disturbing factors, most of which will be unknown.

R. A. Fisher, the noted biologist and one of the founders of modern statistics, has emphasized that many sources of systematic error can be eliminated by *randomization*. Randomization is a process through which subjects are assigned purely by chance to experimental *treatments*—that is, to the influence of selected independent variables.[2] More precisely, the concept treatment is used in the statistical literature on experimental designs to refer to a category or level of an experimental variable. Randomizing the introduction of experimental treatments is a critical principle of experimental design. Let us illustrate what it involves.

In a study carried out in a summer camp for boys, one group of campers was requested to take a test designed such that they would fail, resulting in a loss of their usual movie night privileges.[3] A control group was not exposed to this treatment. Both groups were given identical opportunities before and after this simple experiment to express prejudice toward minorities. The objective was to see if the experimental group (subjected to greater frustration) expressed more prejudice against minorities (as a measure of aggression) than the control group. And in fact they did.

But obviously there could have been a number of personality factors that would also have accounted for the difference found in this study. Some boys might not have really cared about going to the movie in the first place. Some might not have been frustrated by failing the test. Some may have chosen to express hostility toward counselors or fellow campers rather than against minorities. Some might have turned their aggression inward. If each boy had been given the freedom to decide which group to enter, perhaps by volunteering to take the test, even then there would have been no assurance that personality characteristics were *similarly distributed* in the two groups. Perhaps those most prone to expressing prejudice would have volunteered to be in the experimental group, and this fact rather than the frustration experienced might have accounted for the response differences.

One way to check on this indirectly would be to measure the attitudes of both groups prior to the test experience. But such a tactic could lead to additional complications. The intuitively obvious answer is to flip a coin to decide

2.    Fisher's classic work on the subject became the cornerstone for much of modern statistical inference. See R. A. Fisher, *The Design of Experiments* (Edinburgh: Oliver & Boyd, 1937).

3.    See N. E. Miller and R. Bugelski, "Minor Studies in Aggression: The Influence of Frustrations Imposed by the In-group on Attitudes Expressed Toward Out-groups," *Journal of Psychology* 25 (1948): 437–42.

which boys are to go into the experimental group and which into the control group. This is a very simple illustration of what Fisher meant by randomization.

A somewhat more complicated randomization procedure would be the following. Suppose a researcher performing a frustration-aggression study suspects that both intelligence (as measured by I.Q. scores) and age (along with numerous unmeasured personality attributes) are likely to affect the outcome. Suppose, too, that three treatment groups are to be used, one receiving a high degree of frustration, one an intermediate amount, and the third (the control group) receiving none. Individuals could be grouped in trios by matching them according to age and I.Q. to whatever degree of precision is desirable. One triplet might contain persons aged 18 with I.Q.s between 110 and 120; a second might consist of three 25-year-olds with I.Q.s of 140 or above.

Obviously it would be more difficult and impractical to match many variables at once. There would not be enough trios with the right combinations of characteristics, and many potential subjects would have to be omitted from the study. But having matched the groups on age and I.Q., the scientist can be assured that any differences found could not be due to these particular variables. The investigator could then use a random device, such as tossing a die, to decide which member of each trio was to go into the control group, which into the group receiving the moderate frustration treatment, and which into the remaining group. Members would not be allowed to volunteer, nor could the researcher rely on personal judgments or on any other nonrandom factors in assigning them to groups.

What does this randomization process accomplish? It allows us to rely on the *laws of probability* to produce *similar distributions* of all the attributes the individuals carried with them into the experiment. If there are undetected personality differences among the three groups, however, these differences will continue to operate and will disturb the final results. The randomization process has not, in this case, strictly controlled for the effect of personality differences in the same way it has for age and I.Q.

Although it is not appropriate here to discuss the complexities of probability theory, the general concept applies in the above illustration. If each of the three groups is large enough, the researcher could expect that *average* levels of frustration tolerance, of initial prejudice, of enthusiasm over movie night, and so on, will be approximately the same in all three groups. Such a probability statement is based on the same intuition and experience that makes it possible to predict (state the probability) that the average coin will come up heads about half the time, that the combination of seven for two dice is more likely than any other sum, and that bridge hands tend to equalize—over the long run. The major advantage of randomization, based on the assumptions in probability theory, is that it controls for the effects of numerous factors all at one time, without the researcher having to know what those precise influences are.

Why, then, does the researcher need to match individuals on the basis of age and I.Q. in the illustration? Would not randomization control for their effects also? It likely would. However, if the researcher strongly suspects that one or two variables are very significant, it is better to keep them under rigid control if feasible. The researcher needs to do so with as many variables as possible, and then randomize the rest.

This essentially means that the researcher turns to randomization when it is difficult, impossible, or not feasible to hold all causal variables strictly constant. There will inevitably be some scatter or unexplained variation about any curve. The purpose of randomization is to make the scatter more nearly due to chance than systematically related to the independent variable whose effects are being studied. In the example, we want to make the effects of personality factors as unrelated to the induced frustration as we can.

Randomization is therefore a much more efficient device than holding all variables constant, even where they are known. Many factors will be of only minor importance individually, though their aggregate effect may be pronounced. It would be ridiculous to attempt to measure them all carefully and keep them rigidly under control when randomization can enable the investigator to assume that their effects have been canceled out. The statistician can calculate exact probabilities, enabling the investigator to specify the chances of distortions being greater than a given magnitude. By modifying the research design or increasing the sample size, the scientist can gain almost any degree of precision desired, though in general the more precision one wants the larger the sample must be.

### Multiple Experimental Variables

It has been pointed out that randomization increases efficiency of design. There are additional ways to increase efficiency in instances where the investigator is interested in studying the effects of more than one experimental variable at once. In most studies at least two or three variables or factors may combine in peculiar ways. For example, in agricultural experiments it is frequently desirable to try out different combinations of soil types, fertilizers, and seed types. Perhaps a given fertilizer works best in combination with a particular soil type. Or two fertilizers may work equally well on certain types of plants but not others. In such instances, if one were to look singly at the fertilizer types, and then hold fertilizer constant and vary the soil type, and then compare different kinds of seeds, one might overlook the peculiar combinations of joint effects, or what are called *interactions* in the statistical literature. Quite apart from this, the researcher would find it necessary to conduct many different experiments when one might have sufficed.

As soon as one allows for combinations of experimental variables, the statistical analysis can become rather complicated. However, techniques have been worked out for estimating each of the so-called *main effects* (average effects) of the separate experimental variables, plus the *interaction effects* of various combinations over and above the main effects. There will also be random variation, or variation due to chance. Probability statements can be made about random variation, but not about the magnitude of the potential effects of variables that have not been perfectly controlled in the randomization process.

Let us illustrate with a somewhat different example. Suppose a social scientist is trying to study disruptive behavior among children by designing an experiment in a school setting in which the teachers are given different sets of guidelines for dealing with this kind of behavior. Obviously the teacher per se is a factor in this situation, since not all teachers will use the same approaches or be equally effective. From the standpoint of the investigator, the teacher represents, statistically speaking, a nuisance, or *disturbance factor*. That is, the teacher is likely creating real effects the investigator would hope could be ignored. But some teachers may work best with one technique, others with a second. This would be an example of interaction between teacher and method. The investigator might like to be able to recommend that method B is superior to methods A and C for all teachers, but this might be unrealistic. If the researcher finds that some teachers are relatively more effective with one method than another, he or she has an additional task. The researcher must determine why this should be the case. Perhaps it is a matter of experience, training, or some personality factor. If so, the researcher would have to qualify any generalization made, by recommending method B only for teachers with certain characteristics.

Perhaps the investigator also suspects that the size of the class has some bearing on the effectiveness of the method. Method A may work best for small classes but may require too intensive control for a larger class. Suppose, then, that there are three experimental variables to be studied together: the method for controlling disruptive behavior, the teacher, and the class size.[4] If these were studied naturally, as they might occur without manipulation in an actual school setting, one might find the following kind of situation, which is purely hypothetical. Teacher X, who has been teaching for thirty years and thoroughly dislikes aggressive children, has been given relatively small classes. Teachers Y and Z, both new, prefer method C, and there is no one using method B. Teacher Y is intolerant of disruptive children, whereas Teacher Z is

4. Of course, the teacher is not a "variable" in any strict sense of the term. When we speak about the "teacher variable," we are in effect admitting our ignorance as to what produces differences among teachers. If we find such differences, our next step is to construct sets of variables (e.g., teacher's age, experience, personality traits) that can account for these differences.

not. They are good friends and discuss their techniques and problems frequently. Teacher Z happens to have a much larger class than Teacher Y because of the resignation of one of the other teachers.

In natural settings such as this, one ordinarily expects to find the independent variables of interest mixed together or highly interrelated. Teachers who prefer method A may always teach the larger classes, and so forth. This confounding of independent or causal variables is one of the basic reasons why we have difficulties in nonexperimental research. In this illustration we could not separate the teacher effect from the method or size effects.

The basic advantage of the experimental design, in addition to the possibility of randomization, is that the researcher can manipulate the situation so that all of the independent or causal variables are made to be unrelated to each other in the experiment. For example, the investigator may decide to use three teaching methods, four different teachers, and two class sizes (say 15 and 30 students). The essential feature of experimental designs is their *symmetry* with respect to numbers of replications, which makes it possible to separate the various main effects and interaction effects. In this example each technique might be tried the same number of times for both class sizes and by all four teachers. Each teacher, in turn, will have equal numbers of classes of the two different sizes. One possible combination might be as follows:

Table 4-1 **Symmetrical Experimental Design Involving Three Factors and Two Replications.**

| CLASS SIZE | TEACHER NUMBER | | | |
|---|---|---|---|---|
| | 1 | 2 | 3 | 4 |
| Small | A | A | A | A |
| | A | A | A | A |
| | B | B | B | B |
| | B | B | B | B |
| | C | C | C | C |
| | C | C | C | C |
| Large | A | A | A | A |
| | A | A | A | A |
| | B | B | B | B |
| | B | B | B | B |
| | C | C | C | C |
| | C | C | C | C |

We see that each teacher uses method A four times, twice each with small and large classes. The same is true for methods B and C. Looking at it another way, there are no systematic teacher or class-size differences among the three methods. If the mean "disruption" score for the three methods is found to differ more than one would expect by chance, given the possibility of random disturbances, then this cannot be due to systematic teacher or size differences. Similarly, if disruptive behavior is more pronounced in large classes than small ones, this cannot be due to teacher or method effects. By comparing the three sets of means (one for differences among teachers, a second for differences among methods, and the third for the sizes), one can obtain estimates of the various main effects. These will tell us which of the three variables is most important, on the average. Perhaps there is very little difference between the two class sizes.

Although the detailed reasoning is too complex to be treated here, one can also obtain estimates of the peculiar combination effects, or interactions. All teachers but the first might work best with method B. But the difference between B and C might be very unimportant in the larger classes, whereas in the smaller ones B might be definitely superior. If it were suspected that teacher 1, who is more effective with method A, is really more typical of teachers than any of the remainder, then a follow-up experiment might be made in order to learn more about teacher differences. In this second experiment a larger number of teachers might be used at the expense of dropping, say, method C. On the other hand, if class size proved to be more important than teacher differences, a second experiment might involve a larger number of size and method combinations.

An element of randomization should also enter the experiment. If the order in which a teacher taught classes were expected to make a difference, this order might be systematically varied, perhaps by having teacher 1 teach in the order ABCABC, whereas teacher 2 used the order BCABCA, and so forth. If this could not be done efficiently, then the order could be randomly selected. Most important, the students should be assigned to the classes randomly, so that all of the really disruptive children were not placed together in the same classroom, with rather disastrous "interaction" effects of a different kind! It is interesting to note that the effect of the student's personality on the teacher's method and effectiveness has not been addressed in this example. This is because method, and other variables, are *made* to be independent of each other, whereas in the "real world" they may not be.

The elements of randomization and symmetry are of basic importance in all experimental designs. The remaining details can be modified according to one's interests, cost factors, and the like. For example, if one were willing to assume that no interactions would be present, and that the main effects were the only ones of interest, then it would be possible to reduce the number of classes by using what is called a "Latin-Square" design in which the number of teachers, methods, and sizes are all the same. For example, suppose one used three teachers and three sizes (large, medium, and small) along with the three methods. The design might be as follows in Table 4–2:

**Table 4-2    Latin-Square Design Involving Three Factors, at Three Levels Each, with One Replication**

| CLASS SIZE | TEACHER NUMBER | | |
|---|---|---|---|
| | 1 | 2 | 3 |
| Small | A | B | C |
| Medium | B | C | A |
| Large | C | A | B |

In this design we see that each method is used three times, once by each teacher and once with each class size. But each method is not used with each *combination* of teacher and size, as was true for the previous design. Therefore if there are peculiar teacher-size interactions (e.g., teacher 1 works best with large classes, teacher 2 with medium ones, and teacher 3 with small ones), this kind of interaction effect will be confounded with the main effects of method (e.g., method C will look better than the others merely because of the teacher-size interaction). Thus, although this Latin-Square design enables the experimenter to separate out all three main effects with many fewer replications (and therefore less cost), it requires the assumption that all interactions are zero.

The general principle illustrated by this comparison of designs is that the researcher must always make decisions that involve a trade-off between design efficiency (and cost) and ability to test assumptions. Some untestable assumptions must always be made in any piece of scientific research. The major dilemma one faces is how many one can afford to make, as compared with the price of a more complex design that might test more of these assumptions and provide more information.

### Assumptions about the Manipulations

So far we have assumed that randomization can take care of disturbing factors, as long as each group contains a large enough number of cases for random errors to cancel each other out. Just how large is "large enough," however, is a technical question that requires a knowledge of statistical inference. This kind of assumption may be realistic in the case of agricultural experiments on wheat yields, where the wheat does not generally react to the fact that it is being experimented on.[5] But what about human beings? The

---

5. This distinction between reactions that occur when human beings are being measured and those that, presumably, do not occur with plants or objects in the physical environment should not be overdrawn. There are many instances in the physical sciences where the process of measurement may disturb the behavior of the object being measured.

mere fact that they know they are in an experiment, or that the setting is somewhat unusual, may influence their behavior.

Another common problem is that the experimenters may think they are manipulating only one variable, such as attitudes toward the positions of political candidates, when they may actually be unwittingly manipulating several at once, such as sex and ethnic stereotyping, vulnerability to charismatic persuasion, and so forth. These unknown variables may in fact be the ones that are producing the differences found in expressed perspectives on political positions.

This problem can be illustrated most simply by a classic study conducted during the depression of the 1930s, before social scientists had become sensitized to this issue.[6] The study involved the productivity of workers making electrical equipment in the Hawthorne Electrical Company, and the phenomenon the investigators discovered has since been called the "Hawthorne Effect." A group of workers was separated from other employees and their work productivity measured after the introduction of a series of changes involving improved lighting, longer rest pauses, and better incentive plans.

Each time a change was made, worker productivity increased, leaving the impression that each change had a progressive effect. As a final check, the experimenters returned to the original unfavorable conditions of poor lighting, no rest pauses, and no incentive system. Seemingly perversely, productivity continued to rise. The explanation proposed was simply that the workers' motivation had improved not because of the specific changes made but because of the exclusive attention given them by management in the context of the research. Workers perceived themselves to be more important in the workplace than previously.

This kind of experimentation would seem extremely naïve today, and it has led many skeptics to claim that any experiments with human subjects will inevitably be misleading because of the artificiality of the experimental setting. How do we know that introductory psychology students, being paid for volunteering in experiments, will act normally, or similarly to other students, or comparably with nonstudents? These are important problems to which social scientists have given considerable thought. While such difficulties cannot be completely overcome, there have been a number of different approaches developed for avoiding the most serious kinds of objections.

Many investigators will go to great lengths to make the experimental setting seem natural. For example, if the hypothetical experiment with school children were carried out in the subjects' own schools, with their normal teachers, and with no word to the parents that anything unusual was occurring, the chances would be more remote that the children would behave unnaturally. An experiment designed to study a small group might better be

6.   This study and other similar ones are reported in detail in F. J. Roethlisberger and W. J. Dickson, *Management and the Worker* (Cambridge, Mass.: Harvard University Press, 1939).

conducted in a home or center than in a laboratory. Measurements might be taken through regular games, as in the case of children, or perhaps as part of research being implemented by someone completely unconnected with the manifest purposes of the study in question. If the fact of measurement could not be hidden, the true purpose of the study might be disguised by various means. A very effective device has been to insert someone into the group to be studied, with instructions that he or she is to act in a particular way regardless of the outcomes, in order to standardize events without their seeming unnatural.

Procedures such as these create inevitable research dilemmas. One must always compromise between the need for a natural setting, one that will not seem artificial or reveal the purpose of the study, and a more controlled setting that is standard across all groups. In the former, a certain amount of control must be sacrificed. In the latter, a certain degree of generalizability is given up. If research were confined to realistic settings outside the laboratory, the researcher would have to tolerate a lavish array of influences producing unanticipated differences that could lead to results with little comparability. Ideally, researchers would want in this case to commit every scientific and personal resource, short of acts of violence, to holding most of these influences constant, since they would have no way of achieving randomization according to strict procedures. Researchers could only hope that the differing effects of these variables canceled each other out.

A second dilemma involves ethical questions. The research subject must be protected from harassing and potentially harmful experiments, experiments that would be destructive of self or others emotionally, or of relationships in the subject's environment outside the experiment. In many instances, moral issues can be resolved by informing subjects about the true purposes of the experiment after it has been completed. If a subject has purposely been misinformed about his or her test performance as part of an experiment, for instance, the subject must be informed afterwards about the falsity of the score. The problem, however, is that if the experiment took place on a college campus or other setting where communication networks are highly efficient for certain kinds of information, this kind of honest feedback to research subjects could quickly prejudice the research.

An equally serious predicament is that of preventing exploitation in reverse—i.e., preventing subjects from defeating the purpose of a study by refusing to take it seriously, or by trying to infer what the researcher is investigating by studying the study! In this instance, it is essential to find ways to motivate the subjects to cooperate appropriately.

A variety of appeals may have to be tried. In some cases subjects may be paid for participating. If the experiment involves playing a competitive game, subjects may be rewarded for certain levels of performance. In other cases, intellectual curiosity or an interest in the advancement of science may need to be reinforced. Subjects may be given partial course credit for taking part. In addition, the researcher must try to make the experiment as interesting as possible to potential subjects, one in which they can become so personally involved that they are eventually desensitized to their role as subjects and act more naturally. It is an additional task of the researcher, then, to undertake evaluation studies to determine which kinds of appeals for participation seem most effective in given settings and circumstances. It is necessary that some social scientists carry out experiments on experiments.

### Effects of Premeasurement and Uncontrolled Events

In addition to these complications, there is also the possibility that the *initial measurements* made on both the control and experimental groups may themselves affect the outcomes. For example, let us suppose that in a study of the personal susceptibility of individuals to different kinds of environmental stress, research subjects are given an initial questionnaire designed to determine how comparable (well-matched) the control and experimental groups are. Some subjects will have become aware of the purpose of the experiment in this process. When questionnaires or other measuring instruments are used later, subjects may recall their initial responses, and this knowledge may affect their subsequent responses. It may bias them toward making responses consistent with their first ones or toward changing their responses for reasons that are not easily detected or documented.

Subjects' interest in the dependent variable—in this case, their own symptoms—may also lead to greater vulnerability to influences other than the experimental variables being introduced, these influences again being difficult to identify and measure. *Pilot* or *demonstration studies,* whose purpose is to determine the feasibility of carrying out a larger project responsive to the same issue, suffer greatly from this kind of problem. The feasibility study and the full-scale research effort may involve overlapping subjects, or pilot study subjects may communicate with those in the continuing research project.

The main effects of a measurement made prior to the introduction of the experimental treatment can be canceled out by subtracting the scores of the control and experimental groups taken before and after the experiment. For example, suppose the following figures represented mean scores on a symptom scale representing the before and after measurements of the control and experimental groups:

Table   4-3     Hypothetical Before and After Scores for Three Groups

|  | GROUP RECEIVING | | |
|  | No stress | Moderate stress | High stress |
|---|---|---|---|
| Before | 50 | 46 | 43 |
| After | 55 | 54 | 66 |

It could be reasoned that since the mean score for the control group, without any stress, increased by five points from 50 to 55, we could expect that the remaining two groups might be similarly affected by whatever induced this change in the control group. Perhaps this change was due to the premeasurement or to uncontrolled events of which the experimenter was unaware. There may have been so-called *maturational effects* such as fatigue, hunger, or (in more long-range experiments) a learning or socialization effect.

We note an increase from 46 to 54 in the second group. This represents a change of eight points, five of which might be due to the effects attributable to premeasurement or uncontrolled events operating on the control group. Therefore, it could be assumed that the response to stress, in and of itself, increased the average score by only a net amount of three units. On the other hand, in the third group the total change is twenty-three points, eighteen of which could be attributed to the effects of high stress. The investigator might infer that whereas moderate stress does not have much symptomatic effect, a larger amount has a considerable impact.

But the situation is not so simple if there is an *interaction effect* between the premeasurement, or uncontrolled, factors and the experimental variable. Suppose the premeasurement sensitizes subjects who are exposed to stress but not those in the control group. Or suppose uncontrolled events *plus* the experimental variable produce unusual effects that would not be obtained under other circumstances. One way to study the interaction effects of premeasurement with those of the experimental variable is to introduce two additional groups that have not been premeasured, one of which is also exposed to the experimental variable whereas the other is not.[7] Provided that randomization can be counted on to equalize the four groups, it can be shown that interactions involving the premeasurement can be estimated by means of this four-group design. But since it will be impossible to expose some groups to uncontrolled events while others are not, interactions between these uncontrolled events and the experimental variable will always be confounded with the main effects of the experimental variable. It would not be possible, in the example used, to expose some of the groups to additional influences such as a particular personal characteristic of the researcher introducing the treatment, and not expose the others to this same influence. Therefore if something specific to the interventionist or to the research environment is affecting the level of symptomatology, there is no way to sort out these effects from the main effects—i.e., the symptoms attributable only to the specific stresses being introduced.

This is a fundamental difficulty that can be avoided only by controlling the uncontrolled events as carefully as possible. But the more carefully they are controlled, the less natural the experimental setting often becomes, and

7. A very readable discussion of these basic designs is given in Claire Selltiz, Lawrence S. Wrightsman, and Stuart W. Cook, *Research Methods in Social Relations,* 3rd. ed. (New York: Holt, Rinehart & Winston, 1976).

the more difficult it is to generalize from experimental findings to the real world where uncontrolled events constantly occur and describe "real life." Where a study of human beings is involved, some social scientists are skeptical about applying rigid experimental designs to any but the simplest kinds of phenomena. This is a rather purist conclusion, but it is based on a rational analysis of the magnitude of the research problems posed. If the insistence on purism constrains the researcher from even attempting to deal with complex events, it is not at all useful. As a guide and a caution, it is significantly utilitarian.

Historically, experimental social research has been conducted by psychologists working with lower animals, or with very basic human responses such as perception or simple learning. Social psychologists have also adapted experimental methods to small groups in laboratory settings. These latter studies have the advantage of being relatively inexpensive and of being implementable over relatively brief periods of time. In spite of the difficulties with experimental research, these small group studies have produced important theoretical insights for social scientists.

There has been a developing interest in applying experimental methods to much larger-scale social projects involving entire communities. For example, a very ambitious set of field experiments on alternative income maintenance programs has been conducted in several cities in the United States. One encounters certain practical difficulties in some of these large-scale projects, in addition to those already mentioned. Political or organizational decisions often determine which groups or communities receive the experimental programs and which do not. This permits the kind of self-selection that leads to a confounding of independent variables, which the problem randomization has been designed to eliminate.

In avoiding such difficulties, administrators, elected officials, and others involved in such projects need to be educated to the fact that experiments must be conducted according to sound scientific principles if the results are to be conclusive and the money supporting the projects well spent. This means, of course, that if action projects are to be adequately evaluated, social scientists must be brought into the decision-making process at the beginning stages, not after the programs are already in progress. This reflects the most elementary principles of experimental design, yet it is often poorly understood by those responsible for making the basic decisions. In the short run, knowledge obtained through careful research may be politically or organizationally disturbing to its funders or initiators, but in the long run rational decisions cannot be based on any other procedure.

The research process always consists of a series of compromises. At every step, a judgment must be made as to whether given pieces of data, or certain untested assumptions, are worth the extra expense or sacrifice that will be necessary to obtain the required information. If investigators decide in favor of one variable or research design, they are forced to neglect another.

Ideally these decisions should be based on prior knowledge obtained through cumulative research findings. The less advanced the field, and the less certain this knowledge, the less plausible will be the assumptions one is required to make. But *all* research involves certain untested assumptions, frustrating as this fact may be to both scientist and nonscientist. It is important for both to realize what assumptions are being made at each stage of the research process. Such understanding requires a tolerance for the ambiguities and qualifications surrounding findings, with which all social scientists must cope.

## NONEXPERIMENTAL DESIGNS

The organization of this chapter around experimental and nonexperimental designs, while simplifying and clarifying different research approaches, may mistakenly convey the impression that diverse designs can easily be classified into two types. Realistically speaking, this dichotomy symbolizes only the endpoints of a continuum, and most research designs to greater or lesser extent approximate one of these two extremes. A rigorous experimental design carried out in a well-controlled laboratory or field setting is commonly viewed as conforming most closely to the principles of the scientific method, and therefore as yielding the most valid information. This assessment, however, assumes that the theoretical premises are trustworthy, the variables studied are the most important ones, and the methods of data collection and analysis are without blemish.

There is some degree of consensus in the social sciences that the ultimate goal of social research involves a commitment to continued movement toward the experimental design ideal. It is unfortunate that as social scientists have increasingly come to value and develop experimental designs and strategies, this trend has contributed to an ideological division between some of them—that is, between those who tend to exaggerate the value of experimental methodology irrespective of its appropriateness, and those who reject it outright without objectively assessing its positive qualities. As would be expected, where this attitudinal split exists, it is often related to the newness of the area of study, its complexity, the adequacy of the knowledge base in that area, the constraints placed on the research by the political and organizational environment of the research, and the nature of the research subjects.

This disagreement is unnecessary and unproductive. Clearly there are many research questions, settings, and circumstances that do not lend themselves to the use of experimental design. The research problem of interest may have little precedence in prior research or in the theoretical literature, and therefore the scope of the information base may not support such a design. The rigorous testing of hypotheses requires the narrowing of the range of variables studied to those of most significance to the phenomenon being investigated. The scientist must base that selection of variables on the theoretical and empirical body of knowledge available, as well as his or her own experience, intuition, and creative thinking. Exploring and developing general *propositions,* which state possible and likely relationships between a larger number of variables of potential importance, would be a more appropriate approach when knowledge of the phenomenon is in the early stages of development and integration, or where it is of poor quality either in terms of explanatory concepts or the carefulness of the research.

Consider the area of sex-role research, which has flourished with the growing importance of the women's movement and the rapid social change in sex-role values, norms, and behavior. The knowledge base in that particular area of theory and research, although benefiting from research on other related issues, has a limited history. While some of the research on sex roles has been criticized for its lack of rigor, such judgments need to take into account the level of support for previous research and the extensiveness of previous empirical findings. Studies that appropriately investigate a wide variety of variables, as a prerequisite to more rigorous experimental research, should be given reinforcement.

In addition to the state of the art in a particular area, the organizational and political environment of the research affects the selection of a design. The researcher must be in a pragmatic position to carry out a well-conceived experiment, which involves the simultaneous manipulation of a number of significant variables, rigid controls on several more (as through matching in comparison groups), and randomization of subjects to handle a good many of the remaining variables likely to affect the outcomes of the research. If, as mentioned above, there are considerably more variables of interest than can be encompassed by such experimental manipulations, controls, and randomization, or if randomization is a problem, then implementing an experimental design may not be efficient in terms of potential costs and benefits.

In both the biological and social sciences, whenever human subjects are required by the research, it is obviously far more difficult to conform to the principles of experimental design than it is with animal subjects that are powerless to resist manipulation and present fewer problems with respect to randomization. When human thought, affect, or behavior are the subject of the research, manipulation of the variables and randomization require a willingness on the part of the subject to cooperate with the research, or a perceived or actual powerlessness on the subject's part to resist persuasion and manipulation. A subject's motivation to participate is likely either to bias research results in a systematic way in one direction, or to bias them in undetermined ways for which the researcher has no technique for estimating or compensating. Often subjects require incentives to cooperate, and some research projects pay subjects to participate or gain their participation through various means that provide some other kind of tangible or intangible reward. These incentives may reduce the validity of the research and its generalizability.

Also, some research subjects are much less able to *refuse* participation, or to control what research treatments they will tolerate than others. Patients in hospitals, prison inmates, members of the armed services, recipients of government social welfare programs, and students— all are in weak positions of power in their immediate environments. Their participation in research projects is often far less than truly voluntary. In addition to raising important ethical issues, this problem may be a serious source of bias not only for the research process generally but also for the initial choice of research questions for investigation. It makes conformance to experimental design principles very difficult.

All of these difficulties are compounded if incentives for cooperation do not exist in the research environment, or if actors in that environment interfere with the research treatments or manipulations. Even if a random sample of *willing* subjects has been secured, and these subjects have been distributed randomly into control and experimental groups prior to the introduction of the experimental variables, the extent to which these subjects represent the larger group of individuals to which the findings are to be generalized is often highly questionable.

Let us illustrate some of these constraints. A hypothetical example might be a study of the relative effectiveness of two alternative treatments of convicted felons (the independent variables), using recidivism rates as the dependent variable. The treatment categories might be traditional incarceration (prison) and a well-structured residential program in the community. An experimental design would clearly produce the most satisfactory information. However, a critical requirement would be the randomization of all felons assigned by the courts to (1) traditional incarceration, the control group, and (2) the experimental residential treatment group, *prior* to the introduction of the experimental program.

In addition, the experimenter would need to control for variables other than those in the experimental program itself that might explain the ultimate recidivism rates—i.e., variables such as the influence of fellow workers (assuming the experimental program involved an employment and training component), or of visiting relatives and friends whose access to the felon would be greater than in a prison setting. There would also need to be a careful definition of the *prison program* and of the *experimental program,* in order to sort out clearly the unique features of the alternative treatment whose effects were being tested.

These requirements would likely be impossible to meet because of the structure and usual mode of functioning of the criminal justice system. Judges would either need to assign convicted felons to alternative treatments randomly as they were sentenced, or a pool of incarcerated felons would need to be identified from whom random assignment could be made. Judges would probably find it professionally and politically impossible to do the former, and the pool would have already been socialized to one treatment by the prison environment. Not only would one have to separate out the effects of the latter socialization on both control and experimental subjects, but one would also have to estimate the type of bias it would introduce with respect to the experimental group's attitudes toward residential treatment, and the control group's reaction to perceived inequities in treatment vis-à-vis their peers' new alternative. Such biases could explain the ultimate differences in recidivism rates rather than the program itself. In addition, if such treatment inequities were to be protested by strong special interest groups, pressure could be brought to bear on the funder and administrator of the program to terminate the project.

In situations such as these, where there are intractable problems in fulfilling the requirements of experimental design, and where the political vulnerability of the research issue or setting complicates the research, a more flexible approach may be the most effective one, and sometimes it is the only possibility. The major objective of research using more flexible nonexperimental designs is to identify the key explanatory variables from among the large number of possible ones in an area of study where the knowledge base is not highly developed, and to isolate the major relationships between key variables that are likely to explain a particular phenomenon. Its purpose is also to formulate new concepts, measures, and hypotheses that can contribute to future research that more closely approximates the experimental design.

However, it should be emphasized that the term nonexperimental research refers to a broad continuum of research frameworks, ranging from highly exploratory designs to very rigorous ones that closely approximate the experimental model. It is in this context that we will briefly discuss such designs, summarizing some of their main advantages and some of the constraints they impose on the research process.

### Exploratory Designs

The main purpose of an *exploratory design* is to develop and refine research questions for more rigorous study. Therefore such designs demand that the researcher become thoroughly immersed in the data and rely very heavily on insight and intuition, since dependence on specific hypotheses or a relatively small number of variables known to be significant is either not possible or feasible. It is important that the researcher learn about specific phenomena from as many perspectives as possible, and obtain *general* information rather than data limited by a narrower focus.

Suppose, for example, a researcher has had a persistent interest in how Americans define their "quality of life" in society, based on the premise that the correlation between one's tangible objective life situation and one's *perception* of life quality may be remarkably imperfect. We will assume that little research has been done on personal attitudes, judgments, and satisfactions with respect to life conditions, apart from studies using more objective social indicators of material welfare. Where does the researcher begin? The sensible course may be to select a small sample of individuals as representative as possible, and interview them intensively in order to identify the variables that may possibly affect life quality perspectives. Insights from this exploratory effort could then be used to narrow the list of variables to the most significant, and to formulate some beginning statements about their relationships to one another. Subsequent studies could progressively refine the explanation, measures, design, and other research activities. A very interesting study on this subject was in fact conducted. It was a sophisticated survey based on insights from prior exploratory work.[8]

Exploratory designs have substantial advantages, particularly flexibility in producing and integrating creative ideas and setting precedents for further research and theory. A major difficulty, however, is in replicating the research carried out within them. *Replication* or the repetition of a particular research design and measuring instruments at a different point in time (and sometimes within a different setting and with a different group of comparable subjects) tests the durability of the original findings and therefore checks their validity. The less experimental and the more exploratory a design, the harder it is to replicate the research. The research design often influences the choice of data collection and analysis methods, and the methods appropriate to an exploratory design are often difficult to standardize. Sometimes such studies are quite idiosyncratic.

In some disciplines, anthropology for example, an unwritten professional code mediates against systematic replication. Repeating a creative, inventive, and highly original study is sometimes viewed as an insult to the initial researcher's ability, integrity, and achievement. Originality, per se, is more a cherished value in some areas of social research than others. The stress on novel work is a significant norm guiding the socialization of social science graduate students. Replication runs counter to this ethic and is also less likely to be rewarded professionally. There is often a mistaken disdain for "mere" replication research.

A more pervasive complication is that replication is not adequately reinforced by the funders of most social research, who consider replication to be an unnecessary luxury and therefore not cost effective. The result is that replication of nonexperimental research, the predominant type of research in the social sciences, does not frequently occur. One of the consequences is that research tends more to spread to new questions than to reexamine—systematically and sometimes tediously—the theoretical models, variables, relationships, designs, and methods of previous efforts.

A technical difficulty with replication using nonexperimental designs is the problem of explaining any differences found between the results of the

8. See Angus Campbell, Philip E. Converse, and Willard L. Rodgers, *The Quality of American Life* (New York: Russell Sage Foundation, 1976).

original study and those of the replication whenever a second investigator studies the same group, community, or society. That is, do the findings differ simply because the investigator, setting, or people have changed, or because the selection of measurements or the measures themselves have changed? If scientific laws could predict such changes, then corrections could uncover the measurement artifacts. With good theories we might be able to separate real change from measurement error. But the chicken-and-egg dilemma is this: good measurement is needed to verify theories, yet it is often true that the adequacy of the measurement can only be evaluated if one makes a set of *theoretical* assumptions with respect to the *comparability* of measures across settings and time periods.

A practical form of replication involves conducting numerous studies on similar groups to see if similar conclusions are reached. If they are, we can have more faith in the original findings. But if they are not, we must again decide whether the differences are due to measurement error or to real differences. In this form of replication, we are not concerned with changes in the same group, but with variability among groups. If we could assume that all groups are alike, or that they differ in known ways, we could assess the degree to which the differences were due to measurement differences, observation methods, or other factors introduced by the investigators themselves. If we knew there were no differences in measurement, we could determine the extent to which the groups actually were dissimilar. But if we lack both kinds of information, the sources of the identified differences will clearly be in doubt.

### Quasi-Experimental Designs

Research designs at the other end of the nonexperimental continuum are sometimes called *quasi-experimental* because they closely approximate the principles of experimental design.[9] There is rarely an opportunity to implement a truly experimental design in studying certain issues, such as the impact of policy initiatives and social programs. Nevertheless with careful planning, and often a great deal of innovation, the researcher can devise ways to meet some of the experimental requirements.

Quasi-experimental designs are used to reduce the sources of invalidity and the constraints to generalizability. In that respect their purpose is faithful to the principles of experimental design—i.e., they control for the effects of extraneous variables, for interaction effects, and for the effects of premeasurement. However, the means for achieving control represent pragmatic compromises with the experimental ideal. Quasi-experimental designs will be discussed further in Chapter 6, Policy Research, which covers an area of

---

9.   See Donald T. Campbell and Julian C. Stanley, *Experimental and Quasi-Experimental Designs for Research* (Chicago: Rand McNally College Publishing Company, 1963).

research in which this kind of design has become a very important and useful tool.

### Descriptive Designs

On the continuum between studies based on exploratory and quasi-experimental designs are studies commonly termed "descriptive." This term is a practical operational one and refers to studies based on designs that guide the *description* of a phenomenon's characteristics. The purpose of *descriptive designs* is to investigate associations between key variables in an explanatory model, without attributing causal significance to those relationships. Therefore descriptive designs are well suited to research problems based on a reasonable reservoir of theoretical and empirical knowledge, but that cannot be studied easily using experimental designs and methods.

As this implies, descriptive designs apply to a wide range of research subjects and issues: groups, communities, social norms, population distributions, states of health, economic philosophies, the structure of bureaucracies, people's attitudes and patterns of behavior, and so on. They also permit many diverse data collection and analysis procedures to be used. However, neither the designs nor the methods appropriate to them are as flexible as exploratory designs. They require a sufficient knowledge base and careful planning to economize the research effort, protect against bias, and increase the data's reliability and validity. This demands a clear definition of what variables are to be measured and how, and what subjects will be sampled and how they will be selected.

*Social surveys* are a prime example of research carried out within a descriptive design that involves a very systematic, standardized approach to data collection and analysis. Survey designs, and other rigorous descriptive designs, constitute a large and significant portion of social research. A problem particularly relevant to sample surveys, and one that is continually raised in research generally, is again the generalizability of one's findings.

For example, in describing a phenomenon of interest to the social scientist, how typical of *other* phenomena is the one set of findings describing the characteristics of this first phenomenon? How typical of early Indian cultures are the mound builders? How comparable are the data collected by two different scientists studying Western European social welfare systems, and to what other systems can the data be considered relevant? Have these researchers asked the same questions? Are there subtle differences in their working propositions, their intellectual or philosophical biases, or their personal approaches that affect the responses they obtain? What factors influence the way they interpret their data?

In the sample survey a premium is placed on *standardization* to assure that the research is generalizable and replicable. The social scientist using a survey design has three concerns. The first is with the sampling aspects of the design and their implications for the generalizability of the research results. The second is with the collection of data within the design, such that all respondents are reacting to nearly identical situations—for example, similar interviewer relationships and the same sets of questions. The third is with the specification of standard criteria for data analysis, so that different analysts are likely to reach similar conclusions when working with the same set of data. In this chapter, we will discuss only the first of these concerns.

### Sampling Designs

Just as a number of experimental design procedures are discussed in the statistics literature, a number of sampling designs are described in the survey literature. Both procedures represent complex design issues. In general they address similar questions: (1) what categories of subjects should be selected in the study? (2) how many of each category need to be selected? and (3) how should subjects be selected within each category? Sampling designs attempt to answer these questions. The ultimate goal is to produce empirical findings that can be generalized beyond the single study in which they are generated.

As pointed out earlier, one of the problems in carrying out research within exploratory designs is the relatively small, carefully selected samples appropriate to this kind of research, which make it difficult to decide how representative the research subjects and therefore the research findings really are. This problem could be resolved to some degree by replication, but that is frequently hard to accomplish. Descriptive surveys resolve this complication through sampling procedures that are part of the research design. These usually involve a *probability sample.*

The main feature of a probability sample is that each individual in the entire population of individuals to which a research generalization is to be made must have a *known* probability, or likelihood, of appearing in the sample. Before considering several kinds of probability sampling procedures, let us illustrate the general importance of a sampling design. Suppose you have been told on a news report that a survey has been conducted showing that 60 percent of the Protestants sampled intended to vote Republican, whereas only 40 percent of the Catholics expected to vote Republican. Of course, you might want to know the implications of this fact for the final vote tabulation, in which case it would be necessary to know the proportions of Protestants and Catholics in the area. But let us assume that you are primarily interested in this difference, which amounts to 20 percent, and which seems to require some kind of explanation.

What are the questions you should ask? First, you would want to know how the sample was selected. Were these simply friends of the announcer, or were they selected "scientifically"? Another question is: "Do the responses accurately predict the way people will actually vote?" In this case we shall assume that this particular question can be answered by pointing to previous successes in predicting voting behavior from such surveys. The specific question we need to deal with involves the size of the sample. Consider the situations in Table 4-4(A-E). The figures in the body of each table refer to the actual numbers of people sampled. In table A there are only ten people in all, whereas there are two thousand in table E. In every table, however, the percentages of Protestants and Catholics favoring the Republicans are 60 and 40 respectively.

Clearly, one would not have much faith in the generalizability of the results of tables A and B, containing ten and twenty cases respectively. But what about C? Or D? Just what are the chances of finding a 20 percent difference between Protestants and Catholics in each instance? Intuition would be a very poor guide here, although it seems "obvious" that one should have more faith that a real difference exists within the larger population in the case of the last table than in the first. But exactly what is meant by this statement, and how does one go about pinning down the odds?

This is a problem in *statistical inference,* a relatively complex field based on the mathematical laws of probability. In this simple example, the prob-

Table 4-4　Hypothetical Sample Data for which There Is the Same Relationship between Religion and Political Preference, but Sample Size Increases

| A | | | | B | | |
|---|---|---|---|---|---|---|
| | Protestant | Catholic | Total | Protestant | Catholic | Total |
| Republican | 3 | 2 | 5 | 6 | 4 | 10 |
| Democrat | 2 | 3 | 5 | 4 | 6 | 10 |
| Total | 5 | 5 | 10 | 10 | 10 | 20 |

| C | | | | D | | |
|---|---|---|---|---|---|---|
| | Protestant | Catholic | Total | Protestant | Catholic | Total |
| Republican | 30 | 20 | 50 | 60 | 40 | 100 |
| Democrat | 20 | 30 | 50 | 40 | 60 | 100 |
| Total | 50 | 50 | 100 | 100 | 100 | 200 |

| E | | |
|---|---|---|
| | Protestant | Catholic | Total |
| Republican | 600 | 400 | 1000 |
| Democrat | 400 | 600 | 1000 |
| Total | 1000 | 1000 | 2000 |

abilities can be specified *if* the sampling design has been a proper one. But if we do not know how the cases were selected, nothing much can be said. If we know that the sample is a ***random sample***—that is, one in which all combinations of persons have been given an equal chance of being selected—then we may say that if there were no difference in the larger population between the percentages of Protestants and Catholics preferring the Republicans, then the chances are very high that sampling fluctuations alone could account for the results of tables A and B. The chances of getting a 20 percent sample difference in table C are about one in twenty (written $P = .05$); for table D they are less than one in a hundred ($P < .01$), and for table E they are infinitesimal.[10]

It would be very comfortable if we could achieve certainty, but unless we collected data on the entire population this result would be impossible. Given the huge size of the voting population, such a goal would obviously be impractical. But we see from these particular examples that there are some general design principles that make it possible to provide precise probabilities that particular sets of outcomes will result. These, together with any information we might have about the accuracy of measurement, give us a rational basis for evaluating the confidence we can have in the survey results.

One general principle is intuitively obvious. Other things being equal, the larger the sample the more confidence we have that sample results (e.g., a 20 percent difference) will approximate the true figures for the population. Less obvious is the point that it is the *size* of the sample that counts, not the proportion of the population that it represents. This statement is not quite true if the sample becomes almost as large as the population, but it is a very good approximation. If the sample is really a random one, we have just as much faith in the results of table E, regardless of whether the population contains twenty thousand or twenty million persons. This runs counter to the common-sense argument people sometimes raise that surveys must not be any good because they themselves have never been asked for their opinions. It is in fact possible to get very good estimates of voting intentions from a sample of two thousand, even where one is dealing with the entire population of the United States. Naturally, only a small *proportion* of people would be selected in such a sample.

Another common-sense principle is that the bigger the difference found in the sample, the less likely it is that this difference could have occurred purely by chance, other things being equal. In our example we are assuming a 20 percent difference, but perhaps it might have been 10 percent or 30 percent. However, common sense is not very reliable in telling us whether we should

---

10.    Procedures for computing such probabilities in simple tables of this sort are discussed under the heading of "chi-square" in practically all textbooks on applied statistics. The crucial point is that all such computations require the assumption that a probability sampling procedure has been used and that measurement error is negligible.

have more faith in a 20 percent difference with four hundred cases or a 30 percent difference with two hundred cases. Such questions can only be answered by the statistician.

Finally, the amount of faith we should have in a given size difference for a fixed sample size is also a function of the *kind* of probability sample that has been drawn. We will consider briefly three analytically distinct kinds of probability samples that are often combined in complex surveys. In sample surveys where such combinations are used, the formulas for calculating probabilities can become quite complicated.

The simplest probability sample, conceptually, is the *random sample.* In a random sample, all combinations of persons have an equal probability of being selected. This also means that each individual has the same chance of being selected as any other individual. Random samples can be selected by obtaining a complete listing of all population members and then using a table of random numbers or some other random device for selecting them. In practice, this is equivalent to drawing names from a hat, balls from an urn, or cards from a well-shuffled deck, but it is a bit more exact.

Random sampling does not mean hit-or-miss sampling. One cannot obtain a random sample by interviewing the first hundred people one sees on the street corner or by accepting the first one hundred telephone responses to a radio appeal. Think about the possible biases this kind of sampling can produce. Obviously, the person who never passes that street corner or turns on the radio has no chance of being selected. Remember that we must know the *chances* of each person's being selected in order to calculate probabilities. We cannot know this without some kind of listing and a random device for pulling names from this list.

A second kind of probability sample is the *stratified sample,* which also involves a random selection procedure *within* each of several strata or groupings of individuals. The most common reason why we first group individuals and then select a certain number of cases within each grouping is that we may wish to compare the groups, and a purely random sample might not provide enough cases for doing this. If one wanted to compare Jews with Protestants, a straight random sample of two hundred persons might yield only ten Jews selected by chance. As an alternative, one might obtain separate lists of Protestants and Jews (the two strata) and sample one hundred randomly from each list. Obviously, the principles of stratification can be extended to multiple groupings. One might subdivide the population into four strata: white-collar Protestants, white-collar Jews, blue-collar Protestants, and blue-collar Jews, selecting fifty cases from each. There are also some other more subtle advantages of using stratified samples, but this is not the place to discuss them.

Stratified samples will ordinarily not give every individual an equal chance of being selected. In our example, Jews will be deliberately oversampled, since we wish to obtain enough of them to compare them with Protestants. That is, each Jew will have a higher probability of being selected than each Protestant. Perhaps the sample will consist of one hundred Protestants from a list of ten thousand and one hundred Jews from a list of two hundred. Then each Protestant has one chance in a hundred of being sampled, and each Jew has one chance in two. Since this fact is known, however, and since each Protestant who happens to be sampled represents ninety-nine others, whereas each Jew in the sample represents only one other Jew, the statistician can correct for this known bias by introducing the proper weights in the analysis of the data.

The third type of probability sample is actually the most practical one in large-scale surveys. Lists of American voters simply do not exist. Even city directories get out of date very rapidly, and most counties do not have accurate lists of their residents. (Many lists, such as telephone directories and auto registration lists, are obviously biased in favor of middle-class and upper-class individuals.) There are, however, lists of counties within the United States or census tracts and blocks within cities. A random sample of such counties or blocks might first be selected. If the resulting geographic area is still very large, the selected areas (e.g., counties) can be subdivided and subareas again randomly selected. Finally, a random (or stratified) sample may be selected from within those areas that have been previously selected.

This form of sampling is referred to as *cluster* or *area sampling,* and is much more complex than the previous two kinds. Its obvious advantage is that it saves the cost of obtaining complete lists. Only those counties or census tracts that have been selected (randomly) need to be subdivided still further. Also, there will be considerable savings on interviewer costs. In a nationwide sample, it would obviously be extremely costly to send trained interviewers all over the country to pick up a few interviews here and there (perhaps five in Montana, three in Nevada, and one in Alaska). But having selected, say, fifty counties at random, and then selected individuals within each of these counties, the investigator can make each interviewer responsible for only one or two counties.

The problem with such cluster samples is that one must avoid extremely homogeneous clusters or areas. A film made several years ago, about a town in the Midwest that was found to be representative of the rest of the country, resulted in a number of humorous episodes when this fact was publicized. Of course the town's typicality soon dissolved! This is an example of the extreme form of a cluster sample (one cluster) that might be ideal from the standpoint of saving interviewing costs. But such a cluster sample is dependent on the community being heterogeneous enough that all viewpoints are represented in exactly their proper proportions. Of course no such single communities exist, but perhaps a set of ten or twenty could be found. The opposite extreme would be the community that is perfectly homogeneous, so that any one individual is exactly like the rest. Then we would only need to interview one person to know everything; and even though we interviewed two thousand, our effective sample size would be only one! Of course the selection of this kind of community in our sample could lead to extremely misleading results—either two thousand Republicans or two thousand Democrats.

It does turn out, to no one's surprise, that people who live close together tend to be relatively similar with respect to many of the variables social scientists wish to study: education, income levels, political preferences, or prejudice levels. Yet they are rarely completely homogeneous. Therefore it is necessary to weigh the economic advantages of their proximity with how homogeneous they are—i.e., the degree to which it would be unwise to interview more than a small number of persons from each area. As you can imagine, the problems of selecting an optimum sample become highly complex at this stage.

One important general point should be made before leaving the subject of sampling. Once the sample has been selected according to sound principles, it becomes essential that a very high percentage of those who have been selected through probability procedures actually be interviewed and their responses used in the survey. If they select themselves out of the survey for varying reasons, then the probability nature of the sampling procedure is destroyed. Suppose, for example, that 20 percent refused to be interviewed and another 20 percent could not be located because they were not at home at convenient times of the day. Since we would not know very much about these individuals, other than that they refused or were not at home, we could not claim that we knew the probabilities of each type being actually selected (and used) in the survey. All kinds of unknown biases might be introduced into the study. Some refusals will always occur, and it is the task of methodological studies to determine in a general way the kinds of biases these are likely to introduce. But there is no substitute for a response rate of at least 80 percent. This means that interviewers will need good interpersonal skills and persistence in order to locate research subjects.

## RESEARCH DESIGN AND METHODS
## OF DATA COLLECTION AND ANALYSIS

Research designs are clearly critical to the research process because they *direct* the collection and analysis of data, consistent with the explanation of relationships being explored. The goal is to increase the efficiency of the research activities, and assure that the data are relevant to the theoretical model and accurate in describing the phenomenon being studied.

Classifying designs as exploratory, descriptive, quasi-experimental, or experimental is useful for some purposes, but it represents a highly arbitrary set of decisions. This would be true even if scientists agreed on the definitions of the endpoints of the design continuum. Therefore our objective should not be to categorize types of research or design strategies rigidly, but to appreciate the closeness of the relationship between various research approaches and scientific method. Generally, designs differ in the degree to which they meet the requirements of the experimental model. Some determinants of these variations are the following:

—the nature of the research problem addressed, and its vulnerability to political, social, and organizational pressures;
—the scope and quality of the theoretical and empirical knowledge that can be used in studying a particular phenomenon;
—the extent to which the most important variables explaining the phenomenon can be isolated and manipulated;
—the nature of the subjects of the research, and the constraints placed on their treatment within the study;
—the possibilities for randomizing subjects before introducing change;
—the probable degree of intercorrelation among the key independent variables;
—the degree of control possible in holding certain factors constant while making changes in others;
—the likelihood of initial measurements biasing the study's results; and
—the ability to use statistical methods in analyzing data on a probability sample of subjects.

While a range of designs should be respected, given their appropriateness to any particular piece of research, experimental design standards should underlie all research. The more research efforts adhere to these standards, the greater the general quality of the knowledge produced and used.

Exploratory research plays an important role in formulating new ideas, measures, and propositions, which then contribute to hypotheses for testing within rigorous designs. It is unfortunate that guidelines for moving along the continuum from exploratory to experimental research are not well specified, and that social scientists are not encouraged to follow up carefully on the insights provided by exploratory research.

Even if researchers could resolve potential design problems, however, methods of data collection, analysis, and interpretation would still pose challenges. These challenges must be anticipated and their impact estimated from the beginning. If the researcher has not included such considerations in prior research activities, he or she will not be able to compensate fully for that deficiency. A lack of early attention to such issues may tempt the researcher to draw unwarranted inferences from the data, or overgeneralize the findings. Great care must be taken to link design activities with the choice of data collection methods, if the knowledge to be acquired is to meet the researcher's best expectations. Otherwise, the advantages of the best designs are likely to be compromised.

In the next chapter, we will very briefly introduce you to an aspect of the research process that is perhaps most often associated in people's minds with "research"—that is, ways in which data are obtained, summarized, and their potential meaning assessed in the context of the relationships proposed at the beginning of the research.

# CHAPTER 5
# METHODS OF DATA COLLECTION AND ANALYSIS

The greatest invention of the . . . century was the invention of the method of invention.

There are many ways in which data are collected and analyzed within particular research designs. Numerous books have been written solely about methods of obtaining information and analyzing it. The methods range from very simple technologies to quite complex statistical techniques. A distinction, in fact, is often made between *qualitative* and *quantitative* methods, and this sometimes carries with it a differential valuing of the two approaches. The differences are usually based on the degree to which a particular method requires statistical expertise in its application, qualitative methods being associated with the nonstatistical side of the dichotomy.

As always, dichotomies mask a continuum of possibilities and are therefore limited in their usefulness. Some social scientists believe that research should use a combination of methods that comes as close as possible to implementing experimental design principles. Quantitative methods, because they are more appropriate to experimentation, have often been treated as the most prestigeful social research methods. This has created dissension in a discipline whose research problems and settings infrequently afford opportunities to use ideal experimental designs. Much of the debate over the importance of these two types of methods has therefore been more polemical than productive.

Rather than characterizing a piece of research as qualitative or quantitative, it is far more useful to specify the general *methodology* of the study, which includes the research design and the range of methods applied within that design in reaching the overall goal of the research. The critical consideration is whether the data collection and analysis procedures are appropriate to the design, and the design is appropriate to the issue, the setting, and the state of the knowledge base.

There are abundant methods available in the social sciences both for obtaining information on key variables and for analyzing this information. The quality and usefulness of the research findings resulting from their application are greatly affected by the extent to which these methods are consistent with the explanatory model and the research design. A number of alternative methods may suit the model and design equally effectively. Limiting the choice of methods prematurely, because of a lack of technical knowledge or because of value biases, constrains research just as much as if the first step in the research process had been poorly implemented.

There are excellent books available that discuss this wealth of data collection and analytic methods, at various levels of complexity and statistical sophistication depending on the reader's preference and background. Therefore we have been very selective in illustrating this aspect of the research process, and we encourage the reader to plumb the extensive literature in methodology for greater scope and detail. In considering examples in this chapter, the reader should understand that a variety of methods can, usually are, and should be used within particular designs. On the other hand, some methods are clearly not appropriate to certain designs; this should become clearer in the course of the discussion.

## METHODS OF DATA COLLECTION

Enough diverse, fascinating data collection methods exist to tantalize the most resistant researcher. There is a method to satisfy the shyest scientist who adamantly refuses to do research outside the government documents room of the public library, and the uncompromising research extrovert who insists on becoming a member of a Himalayan climbing team in order to study stress at cold temperatures. If only it were as simple as this implies, and the researcher could select whatever method gave the most personal pleasure and least pain! While greater simplicity is one of the goals of research activity, as a *means* it is pure myth.

In collecting data, the main objective is to mesh methods of data collection with the explanation, measures, and design selected for studying a particular phenomenon. This is a very complex task that requires a combination of formal expertise, innovativeness, and careful study of the options. Some studies can be carried out very well using a single method, while others require multiple methods that complement one another or serve as checks on one another. In the following discussion we will cover only a few of the many methods available to the social researcher, to illustrate some of the complexities and possibilities.

## Use of Existing Data

In determining what collection methods will provide the most reliable and valid data with the greatest efficiency (in terms of effort and cost), it is rational to investigate first what relevant data may already be available. Much qualitative and quantitative data already exist, and they may be very useful in measuring certain variables. Data from letters, journals, personal documents, and other historical materials may yield useful information. Data files from previous research may be an important source. A considerable amount of statistical data is accessible from official records, such as census data, health statistics, labor force statistics, and other governmental and private sector statistics collected on a relatively regular basis. A careful investigation of potential data sources—through computer searches, personal searches of compilations of data sources, or inventive searches of less well-known materials—can often identify specific sets of data appropriate to the major variables, measures, and design features that characterize a given research project.

There are important advantages in using secondary sources of data rather than collecting fresh information. Data that are collected on a regular or periodic basis yield information on trends over time. Also, secondary sources avoid the problems of gaining the subjects' cooperation. In addition, the effects of the data collection methods do not themselves alter the data collected. However, there are problems. In using existing data, the researcher should ask why the data were collected, determine the adequacy of the data collection methods, and investigate the extent to which the data accurately describe the variables identified. Some of these data sources are the products of research activity by well-trained scientists. However, some are generated and collected by nonscientists for other than research purposes. The nature of the position held by those responsible for producing the data, as well as the special purposes directing the collection, often shape the kinds of measures used and may narrow the selection of possible measures in a biased way.

For example the U.S. Census Bureau is responsible for collecting a wide range of very important information on the American population. Because of their particular mandates, attitudes, and perspectives, Census administrators ignore certain data: some are too expensive to collect, for example, whereas others are not collected because of prevailing norms or other reasons more difficult to discover. It has been recognized for quite some time that there is substantial undercounting of the Hispanic population, a problem only recently addressed seriously as special interest groups within the Hispanic community have gained greater political influence. Relying on Census data broken down by ethnic status would therefore, at the present time, likely provide misleading information on a number of variables with respect to the Hispanic population.

Because there are always potential hazards in using even the best secondary sources, the researcher needs to make explicit what biases are most likely represented in the data used, and the probable extent to which these biases may affect the research findings. If available data sources have substantial problems, with respect to the adequacy of their collection or their validity, then collection of fresh data is a necessity. Very often it is impossible to find out precisely what the purpose was, what the sampling procedures were, how well the data were collected, or what shaped their summarization, However, using existing data that the researcher has good reason to believe are trustworthy is an excellent method for many studies, and can serve as an additional source of information in combination with other methods in other studies.

In certain kinds of research, an investigation of existing data sources will simply not produce data appropriate to the variables in the explanatory model being used. If this is the case, the researcher must consider what methods, or configuration of methods, will be most efficient and effective to use, given the goals of the research, the design selected, and the researcher's resources and constraints.

### Observation

Observation is one of our primary methods for gathering the necessary information to survive physically and socially as human beings. We take it for granted, unless our vision or information-processing functions are impaired. It becomes a major tool for scientific inquiry to the degree that it specifically explains the relationships proposed between major variables, is organized around adequate measures of these variables, is recorded systematically within a format consistent with an exploration of certain propositions, and is monitored for reliability and validity. Its advantage is that it allows the researcher to document the behavior of subjects as it occurs, and events as they take place. It is not as dependent as other methods on the subject's ability or motivation to participate.

Observation may be *unobtrusive*, as when researchers observe the behavior of mental hospital patients through a specially constructed one-way screen, or *direct* as when they become participant observers in a religious sect. The recording of information may be highly structured and documented in terms of a carefully developed and defined set of categories, or less confined as in some of the richly detailed descriptive ethnographies. The data produced may be quantitative or qualitative. Despite the familiarity of this method in our daily lives and the diversity of techniques, observation as a scientific method requires specialized expertise and strong adherence to procedures that yield reliable, accurate information about the phenomenon being studied. This applies equally to observations made within experimental designs in laboratory settings, and to those made within exploratory designs in highly realistic and fluid settings.

*Participant Observation.* Participant observation refers to a rather wide range of activities varying from actually becoming a bona fide member of a group under study to informally observing and interviewing group members from the outside. The basic prerequisite of all participant observation, however, is that the researcher must gain the confidence of the persons being studied. The researcher's presence must not disrupt or in any way interfere with the natural course of the group's activities, and the subjects must give honest answers to questions and not conceal important activities from the researcher's view.

Anthropologists are probably the most frequent users of this approach, although many researchers in anthropology rely on other methods as well. Obviously, an anthropologist studying a "primitive" tribe for the first time will not be able to foresee specific aspects of any given situation, though he or she may know what has been learned about similar tribes. The researcher may, in fact, have many working hypotheses concerning ways in which variables are interrelated and what he or she can expect to find. An anthropologist would be very surprised, for example, to find a highly elaborated political system or a hierarchical religious structure in a tribe whose economy consisted of hunting and gathering and involved a collectivist system of distribution. If the researcher were to find this juxtaposition of hierarchical religious organization and simple economy, he or she might very well suspect that missionaries or other agents of social change had intervened.

It is therefore almost impossible for a reasonably well-read social scientist to enter any situation with a completely open mind and with no clues whatsoever about what will be found. However, social scientists should purge themselves of as many preconceptions as possible and collect as wide a range of facts as possible. They should not begin sifting these facts and interpreting them until they have become very familiar with the general life patterns of the people being studied.

One problem with participant observation, as you can readily imagine, is that it is very difficult to develop specific guidelines for implementing this strategy. Participant observation depends on the interpersonal skills of the investigator and on the ability to prevent personal biases from distorting interpretations. Given the fact that the situation is wide open to such distortions, either intentional or unintentional, there is an obvious need for replication of each piece of research by several investigators. Before returning to this point, however, let us consider several additional examples of research involving participant observation.

An early sociological study that represents the extreme form of active participation, in which one totally immerses oneself in the data, was carried out by Nels Anderson.[1] Anderson wanted to study the life of the hobo, or transient, and could think of no better way to accomplish this than to become one himself. He traveled from city to city, living in what were then known as hobohemias, flophouses, and mission homes. He gradually accumulated numerous insights into such things as the status distinctions among hoboes, how they communicated, their life style, and something about the stages individuals were likely to go through as their status changed from being an occasional worker to a "bum." The resulting study is still fascinating to read and contains numerous insights that could not possibly have been obtained by a "respectable" middle-class survey interviewer.

Participant observation is ideally suited for studying situations where the problem of establishing rapport is especially difficult. Few social scientists are in a position to become actual members of groups themselves, as Anderson did. They would give themselves away, might have the wrong skin color, or might not wish to engage in the form of behavior being studied. One would hardly expect a social scientist to commit a felony in order to study prison life, or undergo surgery to study trauma. It is often possible, however, to work into the natural setting in such a way that after an initial period of suspicion and curiosity, the social scientist becomes trusted and is no longer an object of study by others.

An early classic study that illustrates the usefulness of this method was conducted by William F. Whyte, who studied street corner life in Boston.[2] Whyte made no secret of the fact that he was a social scientist, but he tried to act as naturally as possible in the research setting he had chosen. He frequented the same places as the young men he wished to study, developed important contacts with local small-time politicians, gamblers, and gang leaders, and participated in the regular activities of one of the informal gangs. The insights from this study made a significant contribution to theories of small-group behavior.

A similar kind of study was carried out by the anthropologist Elliot Liebow in an effort to learn more about the lives of urban lower-class black males.[3] One would expect that the presence of a white male would disrupt the normal interaction patterns among blacks who frequented the short-order restaurant Liebow called "Tally's Corner," the setting of most of his research. The essential strategy was to work himself into the local scene so that his presence was taken for granted and he could ask questions without seeming to be overly inquisitive or threatening. By piecing together bits of in-

---

1.  See Nels Anderson, *The Hobo* (Chicago: University of Chicago Press, 1923).

2.  See William F. Whyte, *Street Corner Society* (Chicago: University of Chicago Press, 1943).

3.  See Elliot Liebow, *Tally's Corner* (Boston: Little, Brown and Co., 1967).

formation from conversations about wives, children, lovers, work, the search for work, unemployment, and general daily routines, Liebow was able to produce a very vivid account of what it was like to be a lower-class black male at that time in that area. His insights from this study formed the basis of broader studies.

In Liebow's research, as in all other research involving participant observation, it is obivous that one cannot study *all* the behavior that is occurring. Eventually the social scientist must set priorities and rank order the kinds of data that are most important and possible to collect. Unfortunately there are few if any general rules for doing this except by analogy with previous studies or common practice. Liebow, for example, decided to organize his data around the relationship natural leaders had with various others—wives or partners, other women, their children, fellow workers, and each other. A second social scientist might have chosen to collect and present the findings in another way.

One of the fundamental difficulties with participant observation is the lack of standardization of data. To some extent, each social scientist is like a journalist writing his or her own story; there is little guarantee that several such journalists will report the same story. As mentioned previously, replication is the answer to this difficulty, but replication is not always easy to accomplish. In general, techniques of participant observation provide initial insights that can lead to more careful formulations and explicit hypotheses. But, as was stated above, such findings are idiosyncratic and difficult to replicate. Therefore many social scientists consider participant observation to be very useful at a certain stage in research, particularly in carrying out research within exploratory designs that can be followed up systematically. Unfortunately, many excellent exploratory efforts have not been pursued further. This is partly the fault of social scientists themselves, for not attempting to spell out the implications of their data more explicitly in order to suggest hypotheses. But it is also due to the fact that the guidelines for moving from such exploratory research to more structured and standardized approaches are not very well developed; and there are not enough social scientists to follow up all the leads that are uncovered by such research.

*Systematic Direct Observation.* Unstructured observation may be a very useful method even in laboratory settings where experimental designs are being used to test hypotheses, as an additional method enriching the data base and as a check on the accuracy of other measures. However, in most studies, even very exploratory ones, the goal of the investigator is to develop a specific format for observing and recording observations *prior to* data collection, based on a previous knowledge of the phenomenon. Although the researcher may have little control over what will be observed, he or she can usually determine in advance what aspects of the situation will be most important to observe and document.

If one is interested in aggression in laboratory monkeys, for example, then recording acts of aggression, such as the frequency of biting or hitting within certain time periods, would certainly make more sense than counting how often they peeled paint from the walls of their cages (unless one of the measures of aggression is extremely subtle). Selectively focusing and refining the purpose and content of observation as the knowledge of its relative importance increases is a rational procedure for posing and answering specific research questions. However, prematurely structuring observation in the absence of a sufficient understanding of the phenomenon severely limits what can be learned.

An example of systematic structured observation, based on explanations grounded in previous theory and research, is Bales' classic system of standardized information categories for recording the interaction of individuals in groups.[4] In the beginning, Bales used fifty categories of information. As his theoretical framework became better refined, and the reliability of data collection increased, he reduced the number of categories to those most significant to his explanatory model. The final set of twelve standardized information categories represented a range of assumed reactions by other group members to a particular member's behavior. The behavior of each member was classifiable within carefully defined categories that described positive and negative "social-emotional" behavior or neutral "task" behavior, applicable across diverse group situations. The categories provided information on several group processes important to Bales' theoretical propositions—namely, communication, evaluation, control, decision making, tension reduction, and reintegration.

Gathering data systematically for specific purposes, as Bales did, raises problems of recording and coding. The timing and circumstances of observation and documentation must be decided. Code names, and often computer code numbers, must be developed for the information categories selected, in order to make the data analysis efficient and to yield categories comparable across studies. The procedures for developing information categories and measuring instruments must be consistent, and observers must be well trained in the use of standardized instructions. The definition of each index, or measure of a variable, must be commonly understood; and standard guidelines must direct the observers' decisions about how to record these measures. Personal value judgments and confusion over how to classify what is occurring must be minimized. Pretesting data collection methods, instruments, and procedures—i.e., carrying out trial runs—increases the usefulness of data collected through structured observation.

### Survey Methods

Some of the complications raised in the preceding discussion apply to different kinds of research using a variety of data collection methods. Poten-

---

4.   See R. F. Bales, *Interaction Process Analysis* (Reading, Mass.: Addison-Wesley, 1950).

tial problems are not confined to studies in which observational methods are the primary data collection strategies. Studies such as surveys—using interviews and questionnaires as the main data gathering methods—are not exempt.

Interviews are a much more flexible data collection method than questionnaires; therefore, what is gained in scope of information must be weighed against the fact that the data are not as uniform. Both methods rely on verbal reports of emotional, cognitive, and overt behavior, although interviews permit observations as well. Combinations of structured questionnaires and open-ended interviews are often used in tandem, to increase the areas of information available. The major issue, however, is the *standardization* of data—that is, its organization within uniform, mutually exclusive categories such that variations and irregularities either in the researcher's perceptions or in the recording of information are minimized.

Social surveys, in which data are most often obtained through interviews and questionnaires, illustrate this issue very well. If survey data are to be accurate and trustworthy, the researcher must have developed a way to ensure that the data are standardized. If a large nationwide survey were conducted, using perhaps one hundred interviewers, and if each interviewer were permitted to talk informally with whatever respondents he or she pleased, one can imagine the nature of the results. Interviewers would produce "findings" that supported their own viewpoints. Obviously, in a large-scale survey a certain degree of standardization is absolutely necessary. In fact, a careful survey involves a much higher degree of such standardization than most nonscientists would imagine.

Much time is devoted to the careful training of interviewers, for example. There will be a large number of practice interviews, with periodic sessions in which the interviewers' problems and questions can be answered. A very lengthy interviewer's manual, containing detailed instructions for each question, must be studied very carefully, and many parts committed to memory. Interviewers are carefully instructed on how to "probe" when vague answers have been given and how to repeat questions so that they appear to be differently worded even though the wording is given exactly as before. They are told how to introduce themselves, how to locate the proper respondent in each household, and numerous other things. As the interviewers' completed schedules of answered questions are turned in, they are carefully checked for completeness, possible biases, or other inadequacies.

The wording of questions is a crucial factor in survey research, and it will usually be necessary to develop several "pretests," or trial runs, before the final instrument is prepared. The interview schedule must be carefully planned to be interesting and not too long; response errors and biases must be kept to a minimum. As is true for experiments, it is often necessary to disguise the true purpose of the interview. Sometimes this is done by asking a number of questions that are of no inherent interest to the investigator, with the important questions interspersed so that their interconnection is not too obvious.

Questions must be carefully worded so that a given answer does not imply two different things and so that respondents with varying amounts of formal education can answer them equally well.

Standardization, however, has a number of important disadvantages. One of the major ones is that the wording of the questions may "force" a respondent to give an answer that is not fully accurate. Simple "yes" and "no" answers are obvious examples of forced choice responses, but there are much more complex ones. A respondent may be given a statement together with a list of five possible responses, then asked to give the response that comes closest to his or her own opinion. But suppose none of them do. The investigator may well be putting words into the interviewee's mouth. Why not let the individual talk freely about it and then attempt to classify the answers?

This is often accomplished by inserting what are called "open-ended" questions into the interview schedule. "Would you mind telling me *why* you feel that way?" The difficulty is that interviewers differ considerably in their ability and willingness to elicit really detailed answers to such questions. The person interviewed may not know why he or she feels that way. Should interviewers assume this and move on, or should they attempt to obtain an answer by probing further? It is likely that in many interview schedules the "open-ended" questions will not be answered, whereas a few will contain lengthy essays. If the latter provide additional insights or interesting quotations, then they may be useful for that purpose; but typicality or generalizability is again a complication.

Perhaps a more satisfactory procedure, and one that is commonly used, is to utilize the pretests for these more exploratory formulations and gradually work toward closed or forced-choice answers that are not too restrictive. For example, if the aim is to provide the respondent with five or six alternative answers that include a wide range of possibilities, the first group of respondents (on a pretest) might be given a completely open question and be asked to write essay answers. On the basis of these answers, the investigator could then construct a set of alternative responses that represented perhaps 90 percent of the answers found on the pretest. A second pretest could then be given that included this list of five alternative answers plus space for additional ones. A skillful interviewer could then probe to ascertain whether the list was sufficiently inclusive or whether it contained ambiguities not previously noted. The final version of the question might contain three of the previous alternative answers, plus modifications of the other two, plus a sixth alternative that had not been anticipated as a result of the first pretest.

The pressure to standardize questions can produce a false sense of security in many situations. Although questions may be worded in the same way for all respondents, this does not guarantee that the questions will be interpreted the same way. Some respondents may consider the questions to be threatening or too personal and may deliberately falsify their answers or refuse to cooperate. Others may not take the task seriously enough by giving random responses or ones that they find amusing or that might upset the investigator. Still others may not understand the wording or may interpret the questions differently from the way the investigator intended. A good deal can be learned from the pretest situation, particularly if respondents are given a chance to react to the interview situation. Did they find the questions interesting? Which ones did they find difficult to answer? Why? Were some too personal? What did they think were the objectives of the study? And how did they think it could be improved?

Experience indicates that most respondents are cooperative, seem to enjoy the interview experience, and appear to take it seriously. They seem to give honest answers to questions that many of us would take to be highly personal. Refusals to be interviewed once a contact has been made are relatively rare, no more than 1 or 2 percent in many studies. One of the major obstacles faced in many surveys is the *initial* resistance to being interviewed. A serious threat to survey research are salespeople who are instructed to present themselves as researchers or survey takers and who later divulge that their true purpose is to sell condominiums in Zermatt or travel packages to Lichtenstein.

Of course, only certain facts can be studied by means of survey interviews or mailed questionnaires. These measuring instruments are best at obtaining present attitudes about relatively simple phenomena. They cannot be used to study actual behavior as it takes place. Frequently a respondent is asked to recall how he or she behaved (or felt) at some previous time, but it is recognized that numerous distortions can creep into such recollections. Most of us could not accurately describe our behavior even on the previous day, to say nothing of estimating how much time we spend "on the average" jogging or reading the classics. We can recall how we voted in the previous election, but we often say that we voted with the majority when in fact we did not. Because everyone is expected to vote, we may claim that we voted when we actually only intended to do so. Since it would obviously be impossible to observe each adult in the process of voting, to say nothing of his or her sexual behavior, the social scientist has little choice but to rely on verbal statements.

Most surveys involve a single interview with each respondent, making it impossible to study directly any changes in attitudes. Of course it is possible to ask a respondent how he or she felt last September, or three years ago, but the recall of attitudes is especially difficult and subject to distortions of various kinds. Therefore it is often desirable to use panel surveys, in which a set of respondents is interviewed at different points in time. Respondents tire of this process quickly and the attrition rates in panel studies are very high. However, it is possible, by careful sampling design techniques, to work out rotation systems so that at each successive interviewing period only a fixed proportion of respondents have been interviewed once or twice before. This compromise procedure enables the social scientist to study attitude change without placing too much of a burden on any given set of respondents.

## Indirect Methods

Some methods of data collection depend less than others on how introspective and self-revealing the research subject is. These methods can be fairly flexible. Projective methods, for example, introduce an unstructured stimulus and document the way the subject interprets it. Other methods may be more structured, such as disguised tests of attitudes.[5] The assumption underlying projective methods is that subjects reveal their basic patterns for organizing reality in the coping styles they apply to projective tests and in the meanings they infer from the test stimulus. In this sense, subjects are indirectly encouraged to "project" their ideas, values, conflicts, and self-images onto the content of the test, whether it is ink blots, word associations, drawings, or doll play. The subject's responses are interpreted within a standardized framework designed to identify response *patterns*. This framework is usually based on theoretical explanations and premises about human personality and assumes the existence of subconscious processes. Therefore, projective tests take for granted that the subject's explanation of the content's meaning is a valid representation of significant personal attributes—despite the content's lack of connection with real-life situations—and that the data collected accurately mirror the phenomenon being studied.

Test administrators and interpreters expertly trained in standardized procedures are a necessity in reducing bias. Most projective tests, for example, are administered by trained clinical psychologists. Aside from the issue of how the tests are given and to whom, however, the distinctively high degree of inference required by this method makes it difficult to identify reliability problems, and raises questions about the extent to which the data reflect "the truth." However, projective tests have the advantage of reducing some of the biases generated by other more obtrusive methods, and they provide information on a broad range of behavior from which important insights can be obtained. They often work well in combination with other more direct methods; they broaden and enrich the data base and act as a check on data gathered on the same or similar subjects obtained through other methods. And they are very useful in investigating certain kinds of research problems, particularly in social psychology and anthropology.

Pictorial projective tests designed to collect data on social attitudes rather than personality have somewhat wider utility in social research. Disguising the purpose of such tests is sometimes difficult and is therefore a serious disadvantage; but the fact that multiple responses are possible increases the probability that the subject will reveal some of his or her true behavorial

5. Again, an excellent basic text, which has suggested some of the major points made in this chapter, and which covers the full range of research methods, is Claire Selltiz, Lawrence S. Wrightsman, and Stuart W. Cook, *Research Methods in Social Relations*, 3rd. ed. (New York: Holt, Rinehart & Winston, 1976).

patterns and attitudes. However, it is often difficult to decide which disclosures are real and which due to the subject's knowledge of the test's purpose.

Projective tests are discussed only as one illustration of a large number of unobtrusive methods of data collection.[6] Information tests, reasoning tests, tests of perception, judgment, and memory, and other indirect methods are very useful in measuring certain characteristics, particularly when combined with other direct methods of data collection. Indirect methods also measure reasonable "substitutes" that are highly correlated with the variable the researcher most wants to study.

With all these methods, the disadvantage is that it is difficult to determine the degree to which the data gathered reflect the "true" variable, and to standardize the analysis of these data, a subject to be discussed in the section on analytic methods.

### Data Collection and Measurement Errors

While adequate measurement is certainly important, so also is assessing and correcting measurement errors in one's analysis. Although the issues involved in judging measurement error are technical and elusive and cannot be discussed adequately here, one essential implication deserves emphasis. In order to evaluate measurement errors, one must have *multiple measures* for each of the important variables being investigated. Otherwise there is no possible way of empirically investigating the behavior of these variables.

Perhaps the simplest concept relating to measurement error is *reliability*, which refers to the extent of random measurement error in a measure, *relative to* the "true" variability in that variable. Suppose, for instance, that random coding and computer errors occur in recording respondents' ages. We may expect that such errors will be uncorrelated with all other variables being studied, and that these errors will weaken or attenuate all correlations between age and other variables, since age has been incorrectly measured. Similarly, some factors may distract an interviewer's attention, resulting in a small amount of random error in the recorded values used in the data analysis. Or if a respondent is asked a set of questions measuring attitudes—for example, toward women's rights or foreign affairs—there may be some items that are answered in idiosyncratic ways by different respondents.

In all of these situations, the measures can be intercorrelated if the researcher has available two or more measures for each respondent or subject. A less than perfect correlation between the scores given by two different observers, or between scores on two parts of the same test, means that some random measurement error has occurred. With two or more such measures it

---

6. For an interesting book on indirect methods, see Eugene Webb et al., *Unobtrusive Measures: Non-Reactive Research in the Social Sciences* (Chicago: Rand McNally, 1966).

becomes possible to correct, statistically, for unreliability. Such differences, however, may also be due to *nonrandom* errors, as well as to "real" differences. For instance, if two measures on the same individual are taken at different points in time, as for example through a second interview or test, it may be impossible to distinguish real change from unreliability. Although the topic is quite technical, it *is* possible to infer how much of the difference is due to real change and how much to unreliability if we collect data at *three or more* points in time and if we are willing to make some additional assumptions about the change processes. The essential point is that the likelihood of measurement errors and the necessity for estimating their extent have important implications both for research design and for data collection procedures.

Nonrandom measurement errors pose even more serious complications for data collection and analysis. Such nonrandom errors are frequently discussed under *validity*, an often misunderstood and ambiguous concept. In the simplest terms, validity refers to whether a measure is really describing what it is intended to describe. Validity is the degree to which the measured value and the true value coincide. Obviously this requires a clear concept of the "true value." This may be a relatively simple question for variables such as age or income, but more difficult in the case of a person's relative power position within a family, the extent of a person's deviation from unclear norms, or a worker's "alienation" from the workplace. Even if two observers agree completely in scoring such an individual so that reliability is perfect, the measure may still be invalid because it does not take into account nonrandom sources of measurement error. Both observers may be equally biased, or two tests may favor one group of applicants to exactly the same extent. The assessment of validity, or nonrandom measurement errors, not only requires multiple measures but also a set of *theoretical* assumptions, only some of which will be testable with the data at hand.

## METHODS OF DATA ANALYSIS

Having invested a tremendous amount of thought and energy in developing a theoretical framework, conceptualizing and measuring key variables, planning a research design, and then collecting the data, researchers must be equally careful in their *analysis* of the data. Analytic methods summarize the data so as to yield significant inferences or insights with respect to the theoretical model. Clearly, analysis must be anticipated in the earlier stages of research; however, these previous steps in the research process are carried out in order to achieve the ultimate goal of meaningful analysis. This final stage of research can be the most exciting, because it is here that the researcher discovers how accurate the initial predictions have been and can extract from any unanticipated results new insights for future research. Yet the researcher must also be prepared for disappointment at this stage. Many expected relationships may prove nonexistent or so weak that their practical implications will not be very important.

A new social program, for instance, that promised to be a breakthrough in social planning, may turn out to be no more effective than previous ones, or quite possibly even less effective. Or perhaps only selected features of a policy initiative or project can be shown to have a noticeable effect on the issue of interest. In the data analysis phase of research, as in all others, the researcher must be careful to guard against personal biases and insidious, persistent wishful thinking. If the results lie in an undesired direction, or the differences are significant only in a negligible way from those expected by chance, the researcher may be tempted to explain them away or to emphasize very small differences as though they were substantial ones.

Specifying general guidelines for analyzing data may prevent researcher biases (or the organizational or pragmatic objectives of the sponsoring agency) from affecting the results. As we have implied, such guidelines are not equally clear for all kinds of research. This, in itself, does not mean that the full continuum of research designs should not be considered, but it does imply a greater need to be alert to possible sources of bias in those types of research in which the principles directing data analysis are least explicit and precise. As a general rule, such guidelines are the most specific in experimental and highly quantitative nonexperimental research, and least specific in exploratory research.

In very exploratory research, such as participant observation in an unfamiliar setting, there are few if any explicit guidelines, apart from the very general admonition to pay attention to as many details as possible initially, and then gradually narrow one's focus once the broader picture becomes clearer. Experience and apprenticeship with trained observers is especially crucial here; but since it is virtually impossible to tell another person how to gain "insights" based on a complete immersion in the setting, each investigator is basically left on his or her own. Some will produce highly insightful analyses, whereas others will produce only detailed reporting from which others can search for insights. For this reason, the "technique" of analyzing such data remains highly personal and is very difficult to communicate from one generation of scholars to the next.

Quantitative data analysis, in contrast, has evolved continuously and is comparable across a wide variety of substantive disciplines, from medicine and engineering to the social sciences. This does not imply that such analyses are simple or straightforward, nor does it mean that insights are not needed in order to interpret unexpected findings or to make sense of very complicated and sometimes ambiguous data. What it does mean is that the principles of analysis can be stated abstractly in terms of mathematical and statistical theorems. Such theorems tell us the following:

—There are better and worse ways to proceed.

—Some procedures produce known biases.

—Some are more efficient than others.

—Certain things can be expected to happen when control variables are introduced in a specified model.

—Probability statements can be made about the likelihood of certain results occurring by chance.

—Some ways of simplifying information are superior to others under specifiable conditions.

All of these statistical guidelines simply give us the *rules* for proceeding. They suggest priorities among analysis strategies, and they help us to assess certain biases in one or another type of measure. In themselves, they do not automatically provide theoretical insights, nor can they turn a poorly conceived study into a successful one. What they do provide, however, is a set of tools that enables several different analysts to communicate exactly what went into their analyses, so that others may check the work. They also help routinize many aspects of analysis and allow the investigator to concentrate his or her energies on the most important pieces of information. Investigators thus have "objective" procedures for ruling out or minimizing the more trivial aspects of the results. Even more important, perhaps, these analysis guidelines—and the accompanying computer programs that implement them—make it possible to investigate an extremely large number of possible relationships that could not otherwise be studied.

Consider a typical example in survey research. Let us assume that 450 respondents have been interviewed, and that certain pieces of information concerning 50 respondents are either incomplete or unusable. If the interviews have taken approximately an hour, there may be fifty pieces of information about each respondent; some of these will be data on single questions that the researcher expects to combine into one or more attitude scales. Even if the researcher uses only the 400 complete cases, he or she will still have a total of 20,000 pieces of information in all. Certainly the researcher could not analyze these questionnaires for insights and expect to generate much more than superficial impressions. The data need to be condensed and summarized so that the really important information emerges. But any summarizing measures that a researcher constructs necessarily *lose* information as well. Therefore the goal is to reduce the volume of information, but not prematurely or in a misleading fashion. The theoretical model should serve consistently as the orienting influence.

Furthermore, abstracting the critical information from the data should ideally be accomplished in such a way that theories alternative to the ones being proposed (i.e., competing theories) have an equal opportunity of being supported by the data. Likewise, there should be an opportunity to uncover totally unanticipated results or complications that force us to qualify our original hypotheses or propositions. And we want to do these things efficiently, without taking too much time away from other aspects of the research project and without costing too much money. In this context, one can immediately see that specific guidelines are necessary. And the researcher needs to understand the basic assumptions underlying these guidelines in order to judge the degree to which they are consistent with the data and the research procedures used.

### Standardization of Analysis

It is clearly not only desirable to standardize data collection and sampling procedures but also the analysis procedures. Otherwise, as we have suggested, the biases of the investigator may again play a major role in the final product. However, many consumers of research are basically unsympathetic to tables and statistical summaries. They want interesting descriptions of real cases and quotations of just what "typical" people had to say. While there is no denying that such case studies and quotes do help to portray the results in a vivid way and provide additional insights, they may give a very misleading impression unless supplemented by numerical results.

In a sense, numerical tabulations are more "democratic"; they involve the "one-person one-vote" principle. Quotations obtained from those interviewed, for example, may be used selectively to give the wrong impression. A few very vocal respondents may be quoted to the exclusion of the rest. When we read the remarks of a "typical" respondent, we must rely on the writer's judgment as to which respondents are really typical. In effect, only part of the total information is being used, and the advantages of careful sampling and attention to selection biases are nullified.

In purely descriptive surveys, well-defined analysis procedures will prevent selection biases in the analysis stage. These range from very simple tabular analyses to complex statistical procedures for combining large numbers of variables into a single equation. Basically, these procedures summarize the data into a small number of measures such as *percentages, means, standard deviations* (a measure of the heterogeneity of the data), and various kinds of *correlation coefficients* that measure the degree to which two variables are associated with one another. If investigators want to claim that high prejudice levels go along with high values of political conservatism, for example, they may provide a correlation coefficient and an equation linking the two variables. Or they may provide the consumer with a series of percentage tables, showing that some percentage differences are larger than others.

One common myth is that the presentation of numerical facts inhibits researchers from gaining insights about the "true nature" of the relationship, which they can experience only by some more aesthetic feeling for the data. What often happens, of course, is that the numerical results do not coincide with the insights obtained by an intuitive inspection of the data. And there is nothing whatsoever in tables alone that prevents one from using intuition to arrive at meaningful explanations of the findings. In fact, a series of tables that give peculiar combinations of results may literally demand an explanation from the researcher that requires considerable insight.

There is, however, a sense in which the proponents of nonquantitative social science seem justified. Many survey reports have, in fact, stopped with a presentation of tables and correlations, with only very brief and inadequate interpretations of what might lie behind the data. They are essentially descriptive rather than analytic. They tell a consumer how one can *predict* voting behavior (i.e., throw together the right combinations of variables); but they offer no means of understanding this behavior or any theoretical explanation of the data. This is not a defect of quantitative approaches per se, but of the rather limited objectives of the survey. The same criticism can often be applied to participant observation studies. The reader is often given a vivid description of, say, the milieu of the lower-class Southern white or the minority corporate executive but no fully explicit theoretical context.

We can argue somewhat as follows, however. The investigator is usually focusing on one dependent variable that he or she wishes to "explain." Sometimes it is a social problem variable such as delinquency rates, discrimination, or population growth. But it may not have been selected with any practical objective in mind. Certain variables will undoubtedly be correlated with this dependent variable. If looked at in terms of percentages, this means that there will be large percentage differences using these variables. If interval scales have been used, there will be minimal scatter about smooth curves that describe the relationship between $X$ and $Y$. Even if these associations are strong, they may be due to chance fluctuations (or what is referred to as "sampling error") in small samples. A replication using a different sample might give very different results. If probability sampling has been used, the investigator may apply rather stringent tests to rule out the chance argument. He or she may also place what are called "confidence intervals" around the results, to give the reader a good idea of the accuracy of the estimates. For example, the researcher may say that the probability is .95 that the Republican candidate will get 56 percent of the vote, plus or minus 3 percent.

*If* the chance explanation has been ruled out on probability grounds, and *if* the correlation between two variables is high enough, the investigator may then infer that there may be something worth talking about. The researcher has located a possible explanatory factor and can then begin the more difficult task of making theoretical sense of the correlations. On the other hand, if none of the variables turns out to be related (beyond chance limits) to the variable(s) the researcher is trying to explain, then it is clear that he or she must look elsewhere. Perhaps the researcher has the wrong set of variables altogether. Perhaps the measurement has been so poor that only improved measurement could reveal strong enough correlations. Or perhaps there are so many factors at work that the researcher will need to study 30 or 40 simultaneously before arriving at a satisfactory explanation. The advantage of quantitative procedures is that the researcher can obtain a good idea of just what potential is in the data.

As already implied, the procedures for arriving at these rather minimal tests and descriptive measures are well worked out. The basic gaps that persist seem to be in two principal areas. One is in the area of measurement, and in particular the problem of inferring mental events on the basis of measured indicators of the variables. The second area involves the linking of descriptive facts (whether quantitative or not) with causal interpretations or theories explaining the mechanisms that have produced these facts. In both areas there is an obvious need for explicit rules that will prevent analysts from giving almost any interpretation they please to a given set of facts.

### Multivariate Analysis

From this very brief discussion of the need for standardization of analytic procedures, it should be clear that a thorough understanding of statistics is a necessity in analyzing complex social phenomena. The array of statistical techniques for doing so are often classified under the concept *multivariate analysis*, or the analysis of multiple variables. These techniques permit the researcher to handle complex explanatory models appropriate to the study of complex issues—for example, models requiring ten to twenty independent variables that are intercorrelated in complicated ways. Relationships between such variables are conceived in terms of mathematical equations and equation systems that allow the researcher to control simultaneously for any variables that have been measured (provided that the number of variables does not approximate the total number of cases for which data are available). This type of analysis is an antidote to simplistic explanations that focus on only one or two explanatory variables at a time and that are often very misleading when applied to intricate research problems.

To illustrate, suppose one has collected comparable data on 200 cities in order to explain their crime rates. It would be possible to estimate the direct effects of, say, each of 15 variables while controlling for those of all the others. If some of these variables are themselves intercorrelated, it is also possible to explain these latter interrelationships in terms of still other variables. The entire puzzle can then be assembled by constructing a complex model to explain not only the crime rates but also the intercorrelations among independent variables. This permits the researcher to assess not only the direct effects of each variable but the indirect ones as well.

For instance, perhaps unemployment rates affect family stability and also school dropout rates, with the latter two variables in turn affecting crime and delinquency rates. But perhaps their respective impact on male delinquency rates is much more pronounced at some ages than at others, or in one racial group than in another. Situations of this degree of complexity obviously require good data as well as training in statistical analysis.

We have only briefly discussed some of the more important analysis considerations in carrying out research on complex issues involving quantitative data. It should be sufficient to emphasize the value of gaining expertise in applying statistical guidelines. As a researcher you should always be prepared to play the role of the skeptic and ask yourself the following questions:

—Have you looked at all or most of the important variables?
—Have you measured them appropriately?
—Have you made the analysis so complex that the research consumer cannot "see through" the density of the factual data?
—Have you oversimplified the analysis by omitting important control variables?
—Have you made too much of very weak correlations?
—Have you tested relationships for "statistical significance"? That is, can you assure the consumer that these relationships did not happen as a result of chance or sampling error?

The answers to these questions should establish the foundation for the interpretation of research findings. While the intent of analysis is to distill from data their "essence" relative to a set of theoretical relationships, the purpose of *interpretation* is to determine the broader meaning of what has been distilled, through suggesting how it relates to the existing knowledge base. It may have contributed new knowledge, confirmed previous knowledge, or produced new ideas, propositions, and hypotheses.

However, it is generally unrealistic to define interpretation as a distinct step in research, as it is often inseparable from analysis. The relationship between the two varies with each study, but in all cases it is necessary to anticipate both analysis and interpretation from the beginning. Otherwise the imputing of meaning to data at the end of this process is largely speculative and frequently wasteful of the research effort that preceded it.

The broader goal of research is to interrelate a variety of alternative explanations and sets of empirical findings from a large number of studies. What is most desired is an *integration* of theory and research, based on the investigation of rival theoretical approaches within a continuum of designs and using a range of methods. This is the most effective basis for improving and increasing the knowledge base of social phenomena. It is also the most reliable basis for the development of social policy, an area of activity to which the next chapter is relevant.

# CHAPTER 6
# POLICY
# RESEARCH

The art of progress is to preserve order amid change and to preserve change amid order.

We have been focusing so far on the characteristics of the scientific research process, and only indirectly on its valuable and intriguing pragmatic applications. We cannot continue to escape the dynamics of social phenomena in the real world so easily. The social researcher must match scientific knowledge and technical expertise with sophistication about the different environments in which research is performed and used. Therefore in this chapter we want to discuss one of the major contemporary applications of social research: its utilization in studying policy issues, or what we have chosen to call *policy research*.

Research on policy issues is of considerable significance. The questions examined by policy researchers reveal the way in which societies solve basic problems and improve general life quality. The allocation of resources such as power, human effort, and material goods and services is based largely on decision-makers' perceptions of what the major problems and possibilities are, and of what actions are most appropriate in addressing them. Therefore the subject matter of policy research reflects the continual tension and accomodation between the needs of individuals and the survival needs of organizations, social institutions, and societies. It is within the policy process that pressures to satisfy fundamental human needs—such as those for income, housing, health care, education, employment, the protection of civil liberties and personal safety—mingle and compete with strong influences sustaining organizational life.

Most social scientists have been interested in studying the causes and effects of social problems such as poverty, unemployment, discrimination, and crime. Policy researchers, however, have focused on the process through which policies addressing these problems are formulated and modified, and particularly on the methods chosen to carry out these policies. They have become increasingly absorbed in studying the effects of *planned* social change, which is consciously designed to resolve a specific problem or test a new policy idea.

In discussing how social research can be usefully applied, we will confine ourselves to a rapidly expanding area of policy research, the study of government-funded social programs, demonstration projects, and experiments.[1] The purpose of this research is to investigate how policies designed to change problematic or undesirable social conditions are implemented through specific problem-solving stategies, and with what results. These program strategies, or social treatments, may be time-limited experiments with new policy alternatives, such as pilot studies testing the concept of a guaranteed annual income, or ongoing well-established social programs, such as social welfare programs providing cash transfers and social services to particular individuals.[2]

It is the role of the policy researcher to contribute inferences and insights, based on scientific investigation, about the feasibility of new policy strategies, or the relative success of existing programs and services, in resolving selected aspects of broader social problems. Although giving greatest attention to the effects of these interventions, policy researchers have needed to identify the assumptions (problem definitions) on which these strategies rely. This responsibility has immersed policy researchers in some of the most exciting social debates in history.

The difference in research emphasis between policy researchers and other social scientists can be illustrated with the problem of unemployment. Depending on prevailing rationales, the perceived causes of unemployment may be quite disparate. For example, unemployment may be viewed as primarily due to imperfections in the unemployed person or in the economic system. Similarly, the effects of unemployment may be defined in terms of

1.  It should be understood that there are many sources of funding for policy research outside government, and that many policy studies are carried out without funding. Also, social scientists do not have a monopoly on policy research. It is performed by individuals with diverse backgrounds and formal training. Many policy researchers are trained in business administration, for example. Unfortunately, some evaluations of programs and projects are carried out by individuals with little or no formal research training.

2.  Examples of such programs are government *social insurance* programs that provide a transfer of cash benefits to the aged or disabled, such as Social Security, and government *social welfare* programs that provide cash transfers and/or social services to selected eligible persons, such as Aid For Dependent Children (AFDC), Title XX, and Medicaid. Illustrations of social experiments and demonstration projects are the National Supported Work Demonstrations, which tested the benefits of guaranteed training and jobs for certain categories of unskilled individuals receiving public assistance, and the Welfare Reform Demonstrations, which tested the feasibility of creating a large-scale public-sector jobs program for AFDC clients.

reduced economic productivity, or in loss of individual productivity and self-esteem. Social scientists would be keenly interested in pinpointing the plausible, as compared with the simply expedient, cause-effect relationships involved in the description of unemployment as a social phenomenon.

Policy researchers would undoubtedly share this general interest, but their effort would be directed to studying specific policy initiatives and social programs that address unemployment, particularly those that propose changes in the condition of unemployed persons. Funding would focus researchers' energies on judging how government-funded employment and training programs, for example, are carried out in communities, and how they appear to affect the employment status of individuals receiving services. The researcher would not ordinarily be asked to assess the underlying assumptions, or rationales, of such programs, for example whether they were planned mainly to address a presumed lack of work motivation, or inequities in education and skill due to discrimination. Nevertheless, competent policy researchers must be cognizant of how consistent the choice of a program strategy is with the definition of the basic problem to which it seeks to respond, and the implications any contradictions may have for social policy decisions.

Because of the commitment to investigate both the implicit rationales, as well as the explicit goals, of policy strategies, policy research produces vital and useful insights about powerful influences in many social research environments and their effect on research activities. Removed from the relatively pure and "uncontaminated" conditions of the experimental laboratory, the social policy arena is a fascinating milieu in which phenomena can be observed and analyzed in all their exasperating complexity, as they occur in social nature. Research of this kind has always been an exciting option for those captivated by the dynamic relationship between science and policy making. The activities of the researcher necessarily occur within a setting endowed with provocative tasks and challenges, providing an important illustration of how social research principles can be applied productively to issues emerging from the ongoing life of societies.

Our purpose is to describe the major characteristics, problems, and potentialities in this area of policy research. In the process, we want to stress how difficult it is to apply scientific methods to constantly changing social phenomena that involve the interaction of many diverse variables, over which the researcher has only limited influence, and that operate in settings where the researcher is not the prominent powerholder.

## CHARACTERISTICS OF POLICY RESEARCH

Policy research funds are usually distributed on the basis of an open-bid process, through which the research funder requests specific research proposals. An example might be the need to evaluate the effects of federal maternal and child health services on the health status of rural families. Such funding requests often restrict the time within which research proposals are to be developed, assessed, and selected. They frequently specify narrow research goals and contain quite specific expectations for what is to be studied. They often limit the time between the initiation and completion of the research and their budget options are fairly circumscribed.

Those who formulate the initial version of the research question, on the basis of which the researcher then submits a proposal for funding, and those who set the priorities for what is expected of the research, are often not researchers. The final decisions in awarding research contracts are therefore frequently based on nonscientific criteria, rather than objective research quality.

All of these conditions place serious limitations on policy research at the outset. They favor pragmatic decisions consistent with the current needs and concerns of agencies, usually in the shadow of Congressional judgments of their adequacy. Proposals that suggest the research can be accomplished quickly and inexpensively, and that respond to agency anxieties usually have a better chance of being funded. Sometimes these preferences are short-sighted or address only a few aspects of a much more complex problem. Research meeting such needs may involve a constricted set of variables, fragmenting research efforts across varying problems and issues, and sometimes diverting effort from longer-term, better-planned projects focusing on more central concerns.

Once funded, the policy researcher must live with the fact that the theoretical explanations that guide the research, and the initial statements of the research problem, have been generated by key actors elsewhere. These definitions are created within the political process, through which policies are developed, selected, and applied in a context of competing special interests, rather than by the researcher based on a study of an established body of scientific knowledge. Such political influences often inhibit the development of adequate explanatory models, valid measures of variables, sound experimental designs, reliable methods of data collection, and methods of analysis that are comprehensive enough to produce inferences useful to science and to policy. However, the demands placed on researchers to compensate for these constraints have at the same time stimulated the development of research innovations unique to the study of social phenomena under these realistic conditions.

Several interesting features of policy research are important to emphasize: its history, its relationship to other areas of research less influenced by the vagaries of organizational life, the research issues to which it gives greatest attention, and the characteristics of the research environment.

### History

The strong interest in policy research in the United States has been remarkably recent. The current trend to document how well the objectives of tax-supported social programs have been achieved has evolved quite rapidly. This development was encouraged initially by perceptions that the private business and industrial sector had failed to resolve the severe social problems of the 1930s and early 1940s, and by the subsequent swift growth of government budgets and bureaucracies in response to public demands that elected officials take responsibility for the larger issues of inequitable, unjust, or otherwise unacceptable social conditions.

Such government activities were undoubtedly enhanced by unprecedented economic growth and affluence, which permitted a number of important forces to converge. Among them, an expanding economy offered a broadened tax base in the presence of increasingly articulate pressures from powerful special interest groups. The general level of education and social awareness of the American public, and its growing insistence that government activities remain accessible to public scrutiny, fused with significant advances in computer technology and research methodology.

These and related influences led to a somewhat unexpected use of research expertise to weigh the benefits of social welfare activities against increasing costs. This augmented respect for the role of policy research in determining the value of social welfare activities resulted in a phenomenon worthy in itself of research attention: the so-called "accountability" movement. A consequence of this now well-entrenched public philosophy is that a desire for scientific proof of the effectiveness of existing social programs, and more systematic assessment of the impact of new policy initiatives and innovations, is likely to provide ever-increasing ideological support for policy research, irrespective of the differing levels of funding it may receive.[3]

Ironically, as government acceptance of this investment in research has become more rewarding to social researchers, stimulating a professionalization of policy research, the risks have increased that policy research will be held hostage by the social, political, and organizational priorities of those ultimately in control of resources. In fact, the growing politicization of policy research, and its evolving entrepreneurial character, represent some of the most serious barriers to an appropriate application of research principles to policy issues, and to a rational use of its more reliable findings.[4]

3.  The recent political redefinition of the role of the federal government, represented by the transfer of substantial fiscal and program planning responsibility to the states, the reduction in federal regulations, and the shrinkage of federal research budgets will undoubtedly affect the way in which quality control over the use of program funds is maintained. However, the social and political changes supporting the insistence on proof that costs are warranted by program results will not fade away.

4.  The erosion of the growing dependence of researchers on federal funding may indirectly benefit policy research by encouraging greater discretion and flexibility in the choice of research questions and the analysis of the rationales for policy decisions.

### Distinctiveness

What most distinguishes policy research from research activities in other contexts is its difficulty with two central research requirements: (1) maintenance of control over the *conduct* of research activities—or the degree of autonomy afforded the researcher; and (2) conformance to the principles of scientific method—or the ability of the researcher to *control* and *manipulate* key variables. Autonomy and control are substantially restricted by the social, political, and organizational forces operating within the policy environment and within the specific settings in which data need to be collected. These constraints are evident in other sources of differences as well, such as the following:

—the purposes of the research,
—the selection and formulation of the research question,
—the extent of the limitations placed on the application of experimental design procedures,
—the nature of the research subjects,
—the expectations for research quality by the funder,
—the importance of the constituencies to which the researcher is accountable,
—the ethical issues raised,
—the range of nonresearch skills required,
—the degree of utilization of research findings, and
—the range of opportunity to affect social policy.

While oversimplifying reality, we can make some qualified generalizations about these differences. For example, the purposes underlying policy research are usually more political than scientific. The theoretical assumptions that direct the research tend to emerge dramatically from the social policy process rather than logically from the social science knowledge base. The funders of policy research, rather than the researchers, typically assume responsibility for the initial definition of the research issue to be studied and the specific questions to be investigated. Rather than generating a set of relationships based on previous research, and developing a design tailored to its exploration, the researcher "inherits" an explanation (often unstated) generated in a distinctly different context and is obligated to construct a design and methods with only a partial knowledge of the original premises. In addition, the funder's concerns are not primarily intellectual or scientific, therefore the expectations for research adequacy are not always stringent.

Even if funders were more rigorous, the policy researcher would find the constraints in applying experimental design principles far greater than in other kinds of research, even in the best-conceived social experiments. Too many influences remain under the control of other important actors with different priorities.

As if this were not enough, the researcher's ability to select the subjects of the research according to acceptable sampling principles is severely curtailed by their characteristics. In policy research, the objects of study tend to exhibit "problem" conditions—i.e., the extreme end of a continuum of possibilities. These populations of clients—for example, criminal offenders, the mentally or physically ill, victims of crime, the handicapped, or those stigmatized and discriminated against—are to some extent research captives. They are relatively powerless to resist being studied. Those at the other extreme of the continuum—such as gifted children, illness-free elderly, or successful women executives—are only slightly less vulnerable. This has implications for the validity of policy research data, and also for ethical issues related to the treatment of research subjects.

There may be more serious ethical problems in performing policy research activities generally. Tensions between conflicting research purposes, and competing loyalties to funders, administrators, and the clients of social programs force uneasy choices between the norms and practices of the policy and academic communities. Some of the programs evaluated clearly involve questionable manipulation of clients to satisfy more basic system-sustaining purposes. Some of the assumptions the researcher must take for granted may reflect less than humanitarian visions of life quality.

It is obvious that the policy researcher acquires a wide range of knowledge and a diverse repertoire of skills, independent of a required knowledge of the content area and the expected technical research expertise. An academic knowledge of organizational theory and behavior is a necessity, sophisticated interpersonal skills are extremely useful, and a sense of professional ethics is essential. Finally, policy research findings are more likely to be misused or underutilized than in other areas of social research. They are more susceptible to selective use for political or organizational purposes, and to outright suppression if they run counter to strong ideological pressures. And the extensive qualifications that must often accompany policy results sometimes reduce their credibility and usefulness in the scientific community.

Despite these differences from other social research, policy research must be viewed as an integral part of a range of research options. These options vary from research contexts in which the primary purpose is to contribute to an accumulating body of theory and empirical findings through rigid adherence to scientific method, to contexts in which the major intent is to improve the quality of policy decisions and the solution of social problems through more flexible applications of scientific method. Underlying this diverse and abundant set of research alternatives are common research principles, standards, processes, tasks, and skills.

### Research Issues Addressed

The issues to which policy research must often be responsive, because of the needs, orientations, and priorities of research funders, are frequently narrow and specialized. Rather than focusing, for example, on why so many

Americans are identified as "mentally ill," the policy researcher more likely investigates what effect certain kinds of "mental health services" have on particular categories of mentally ill clients. Often the emphasis is on only selected effects. Few policy researchers would be consciously funded, for instance, to study how mental health services may inadvertently *increase* the psychological problems of clients, even though the unanticipated consequences of social programs are legitimate issues for social researchers generally.

Policy issues reflect a natural preoccupation with the efficacy of specific, often time-limited solutions to politically troublesome emergent problems, rather than with the saliency of broader explanations of longer-developing influences that produce, sustain, or minimize larger social problems. Typically chosen for exploration are special aspects of these more complicated problems, and only certain alternative methods for resolving them. This may occur at the expense of theoretical frameworks that systematically link these specific research projects with the results of previous research, and that include a sufficient range of potential explanatory variables to adequately examine the more restricted research questions chosen. Lacking such a framework, and taking the funder's very specific research expectations for granted, the policy researcher is sometimes in some jeopardy in not being able to identify conflicts between the statement of the basic problem and the selection of program strategies.

For example, the formal purpose of the evaluation component of the 1980 Welfare Reform Demonstrations was to test whether sufficient numbers of minimum wage jobs could be created in communities to permit employable welfare recipients to essentially cover the cost of their government grants. The underlying intent of this job creation effort was to decrease the federal welfare budget. While the research designs were admirable, the definition of the basic problem to which this work strategy was addressed was not a major research concern. The *implicit* problem definition projected the traditional ideology that welfare recipients are in large part responsible for their own undesirable condition, and that strong, mandatory work requirements are necessary to encourage their independence from government subsidies. This was not to suggest that other definitions of the general problem were unavailable, such as the multiple barriers to employability experienced by clients, discrimination, or characteristics of the economy.

Taking the basic intent of the program treatments for granted and assuming the validity of the first definition of the problem, without building into the evaluation the potential explanatory variables in the second definition, the researcher might be tempted to equate the effective generation of jobs with a successful strategy to reduce federal welfare expenditures and increase the motivation of low-income people to work. This may be seriously at odds with reality. If minimum wage work does not alter clients' occupational marketability, and the economy can absorb only so many unskilled workers at wages that support their families, then welfare budgets will not necessarily be reduced in the long run, and may in fact increase. And rising expectations for guaranteed work on the part of these clients, followed by the inability to sustain employment, may in total have a negative effect on their motivation to work. The lesson to be learned is that policy researchers have a very difficult task incorporating key causal variables into the evaluation of specific programs, and must continually sensitize themselves to this problem.[5]

Within this general context, policy researchers are primarily involved in evaluations of social projects and programs that focus on the characteristics of the agencies or organizations providing programs and services, the service consumers themselves, or on the community settings in which the services are transferred from the provider to the individual recipient. By *program evaluation*, we mean the objective, systematic, scientific assessment of programs and projects, ultimately to determine whether the effects measured are consistent with the program's intent, and whether these effects can be attributed to the program itself or to other factors. On this basis, it is expected that more rational decisions can be made about which solutions, strategies, or means are better than others, and about how programs can be improved.

Within this overall purpose, there are two important aspects of social innovations and programs that policy researchers typically evaluate. One is the *process* through which abstract concepts and plans are translated into pragmatic operational social experiments, demonstrations, and programs in realistic environments. This is often termed an evaluation of the *program implementation process*. The other aspect is the *consequences* of program implementation, or the effect a program has on the service provider, consumer, and sometimes the setting in which this significant exchange takes place. This is often called an evaluation of *program impact*.

Competent evaluations will involve a study of both process and impact, since they are highly interrelated. However, since the allocation of policy research funds has often been dependent on Congressional perceptions of researchable issues, the priority has been to encourage impact evaluations. They are viewed as providing quicker and more direct answers to whether or not a program is successful. Even though it is likely that nonprogram variables, operating within the process through which programs are carried out, may often be more responsible for program effects than the service interventions themselves, it has been only recently that research on implementation issues has received serious attention.[6] However, one of the unfortunate

5. As in the medical profession, if the problem has not been accurately diagnosed, the patient may well succumb despite extraordinary efforts to apply certain treatments or may experience a total cure in spite of them. It is a characteristic of policy research that researchers are rarely rewarded for trying to diagnose the disease. They are too often confined to studying incremental changes in the choice of medications.

6. An excellent resource on the evaluation of program implementation is Walter Williams and Richard F. Elmore's *Social Program Implementation* (New York: Academic Press, 1976).

side-effects of the new interest in implementation is that the two kinds of evaluations are frequently done independently of one another and the valuable opportunity to integrate the findings may be sacrificed.

In investigating process and impact, policy researchers are influenced by the fondness of research contractors for two concepts: *efficiency* and *effectiveness*. Efficiency is a quality describing process. It is more often a function of the effort and monetary cost invested in carrying out a program. It may be measured in terms of the quality or quantity of activities the organization responsible for implementing the program engages in, such as planning and allocating funds, overseeing program performance, managing the service delivery system, or interacting directly with clients receiving the services of the program. It may also be measured intangibly, on the basis of the level of staff commitment and morale, or very concretely through the sheer volume of activity in the system (numbers of clients "processed"). In most instances, however, the most acceptable measures of efficiency are those that can be converted easily to dollars, such as "cost per unit of service provided."

In studying the efficiency of a program providing marital counseling services associated with divorce courts, for example, the researcher might want to look for evidence of efficiency in the average length of time between client requests for service and the program's response, the extent to which correct procedures are followed, the conformance of case records to the proper format, the level of consistency between the complexity of the counseling tasks and the professional competence of the staff. However, one of the most cogent indications of efficiency, from the funder's point of view, might be the number of families reunited, in the context of the costs of administration and staff hours required for the average case.

Evaluations of efficiency speak to whether the means selected to resolve a problem justify the dollar costs of the strategy, by comparison with alternative means. The problem with the current emphasis in evaluating efficiency is that too often the long-term social and monetary costs of *not* using a particular strategy are ignored, and the benefits achieved that are not easily translatable into dollar savings are not considered.[7] In addition, alternative strategies for resolving similar problems—such as different ways to preserve the intactness of families other than counseling attached to divorce courts—are usually not evaluated using the same indices for measuring goal achievement. Consequently it is difficult to judge the comparative efficiency of different means.

Effectiveness is a quality attributed to program impact, or the outcomes of programs. It is a function of the change occurring in those participating in

---

7.   Relevant to this issue of broader exploration of costs and benefits is a very competent, innovative discussion of cost-benefit and cost-effectiveness analyses, and their relationship to resource allocation, in Peter H. Rossi, Howard Freeman, and Sonia Wright's, *Evaluation: A Systematic Approach* (London: Sage Publications, 1979).

the program as clients or consumers, and/or change in the status of the service provider. The commitment to change is an integral part of social policy, irrespective of how limited or radical the change may be. The basic assumption on which social programs rest is that a situation exists requiring, for whatever reasons, deliberately designed change. The intent is to *create* a causal relationship between certain treatments and effects. It is this complex set of relationships between the social program interventions or treatments (the independent variables) and the life quality or organizational statuses to be changed (the dependent variables), to which the label "effective" or "ineffective" is then attached.

The critical measures of effectiveness are therefore the differences between the conditions and statuses of the recipients of planned change *before* and *after* the change is introduced, holding other plausible explanations for the alteration of these conditions constant. Again, because of narrowed expectations for how these before-after differences are to be measured and valued, indices of effectiveness have tended to rely on short-term outcomes, and those effects that are most easily described. This has emphasized effects beneficial to the provider over those that involve life quality changes for the client. Also, judgments of effectiveness have often been made without adequate consideration for other explanations of these effects. When this occurs, the assessment of effectiveness can be very arbitrary and capricious. Unintended consequences of the treatments, as well as additional independent variables, will inevitably be neglected in the conceptualization and measurement of important relationships.

The Work Incentive Program (WIN), for example, provides mandatory jobs and training to employable welfare clients. Its purpose is to decrease welfare dependency through requiring work, or training in preparation for work. It has been continually reevaluated over its relatively long legislative history with increasing research sophistication. For many years the national WIN office reported the efficiency of the program to Congress in the form of simple frequency counts, such as numbers of persons registered, or numbers whose employability was appraised in order to select services appropriate to them. The measures of effectiveness were, again, simple counts of individuals who found and retained regular jobs for a least thirty days after leaving the program (irrespective of whether they found them as a result of the program), and the amount of immediate savings realized by the welfare system as a result of terminations from the program (irrespective of whether they were due to residential mobility, remarriage, illness, death, or to a job at sufficient wages). These savings did not take into account potential increased caseload pressures on other social agencies, nor any repetitive movement of clients in and out of the WIN/welfare system.

In the absence of measures of economic, labor force, demographic, and other variables, WIN's funding was determined mainly by "volume-of-activity" measures of efficiency and very limited, immediate measures of effectiveness, independent of economic conditions. After a number of comprehensive, as well as selective evaluations of WIN, more complex definitions of these two concepts evolved, resulting in a more complicated but rational and equitable allocation formula for WIN funds. Congress began to appreciate WIN's longer-term costs and benefits, given the many needs of WIN clients, the restricted job-finding environments in which they sought employment, and the impact of underserved WIN clients on other service providers.

If an evaluation is to be truly comprehensive, it should study both process and impact, both efficiency and effectiveness. However, none of the variables that describe these different program dimensions can be adequately studied in isolation from one another. Their interactive effects are enormously important, if difficult, for the researcher to sort out. Therefore these concepts that are hallmarks of program evaluation must be viewed in perspective. They are arbitrary boundaries, and their scientific usefulness in pursuing basic research purposes is uneven.

Several additional points should be made about the research issues that capture the major time and effort of policy researchers. Although treatments and outcomes are formulated in cause-and-effect terms, and policy makers often expect research to provide cause-and-effect answers, evaluations can only identify the *strengths* and *weaknesses* of social innovations and programs, given the changes desired. In policy research there are clearly more serious barriers to investigating and making inferences about causality than elsewhere. This is often misunderstood by nonresearchers who seek definitive answers from research about the "success" or "failure" of programs. On the basis of these answers they intend to set priorities for continuing or eliminating programs, improving organizational processes and services, promoting or discouraging program strategies, and deciding what policy initiatives ought to be applied more widely.

Many program evaluations yield "negative" results—that is, the program is not considered to be achieving its intent. This is not surprising in the context of a number of policy research problems. The *theories* of change implied in social programs are simplistic. They often assume that very small changes will have relatively large effects. Providing a limited amount of milk, eggs, and cheese to pregnant mothers and children in selected poor families, for instance, is assumed to significantly reduce the debilitating effects of low-protein diets on the brain-cell development of poor children, when in fact the problem is far more complex and the realistic impact of such a program on that problem is potentially small.

Anticipated effects are often evaluated prematurely. The collection of long-term follow-up measures on those exposed to planned change is not usually funded. Yet the effects of many education programs, for example, will not be immediate. Important discrepancies occur between the "ideal" set of program treatments and effects described in the original authorizing legislation, and the "real" set that results from the inevitable redefinition of initial goals and strategies in operating and maintaining the program. Yet the program is often held accountable for the former.

The *magnitude* of expected change is frequently not specified in the original statement of program intent. Realistically, the researcher will observe only limited differences in client characteristics before and after the introduction of the program. This is because the complexity of the problem overwhelms the limited program treatments. It is therefore essential that the research design permit a study of the *significance* of these small differences, if the program is to be judged objectively. A prerequisite is to identify as precisely as possible the *strength* of the treatments proposed, and the *degree* of the effects expected. Conceptual, organizational, political, and sometimes ethical constraints will make this difficult. Nevertheless the program's description must be qualified prior to carrying out the research, if the potential users of policy research are to fully understand the meaning of the findings.

Some criminal justice programs designed to substantially reduce recidivism, for instance, do not eliminate the further involvement of program recipients with law enforcement agencies or the courts, and are therefore judged largely unsuccessful. The *amount* of program resources, apart from their characteristics or quality, may have been insufficient to address the degree of change called for, especially in clients who have complex problems of which criminal behavior may be one presenting symptom. However these programs may produce smaller changes in such individuals that are significant. These incremental changes can affect their more basic problems over time or influence their family and peer relationships.

Actually, there are several points at which the research process may *predispose* programs to biased judgments, either negative or positive. One is in the conceptualization stage, where goals and treatments may not be clearly enough defined. For example, in a child care program, the *ways* in which children are to be benefitted may be quite ambiguous. Another is in the measurement process, where indices describing treatments and effects may not adequately represent the key variables. For instance, in a program intended to organize welfare recipients into a lobbying coalition, the measures of the organizational strategies used and lobbying outcomes to be achieved may not be made explicit. Or the problem may be in the design phase, where adequate controls are not incorporated for holding constant the effects of other nonprogram variables. In a project to place unemployed workers in jobs, for example, there may be no plan to measure variables such as labor market conditions or the characteristics of the labor force.

Or perhaps the sampling methods do not guarantee that the collection of data on the program's clients will truly represent those intended to be exposed to the program—i.e., the clients may easily "self-select" themselves into social experiments. Problems can also occur in the analysis stage, where data collection methods may not be appropriate either to the nature of the needed data or to the subjects. In a culturally sensitive program where indirect methods may be superior, and insensitivity to the attitudes of research subjects will likely create resistance, the data may be too biased to be usable.

The ultimate policy judgments that place planned change efforts on a continuum from success to failure are quite tentative and require extensive qualification. Social innovations and programs judged successful may simply be the product of vague definitions of ideas, low aspirations for change, or inadequate research. On the other hand, poor conceptualization may prejudice programs to failure. Faulty research can also do it. And the changes hoped for may be unrealizable, given the level of resources allocated and the complexity of the problems experienced by individuals and social systems. It is the purpose of competent policy researchers to provide a better basis than this for making such judgments.

## CHARACTERISTICS OF THE POLICY RESEARCH ENVIRONMENT

The uniqueness of policy research lies in its relationship to the intense environment in which policy issues are negotiated, significant policy decisions made, and specific ways devised to implement them. The exchange of power and resources within this environment reveals the potent social, political, and organizational forces that direct its consequences. Researchers interested in exhilarating challenges find in this policy drama an exceptional opportunity to study social science variables in a demandingly realistic setting. Policy research tests not only the researcher's formal scientific education and expertise but his or her creativity in resolving research problems.

With this in mind, we should understand the similarities between the "ideal" policy process and the "ideal" research process. In both cases a series of tasks forms stages, some logically prerequisite to others. Each stage involves a cluster of interrelated administrative, policy, and research tasks. These are frequently referred to as *policy analysis, policy formulation, program implementation, program monitoring, planning and program design, program evaluation,* and the *feedback* of insights from monitoring and evaluation to policy analysis.[8] Of course, neither research nor policy activities rigidly conform to such rational models. The real policy process is an ever-changing cycle, in which diverse influences intervene at critical decision points

8.  Policy analysis is the study of existing knowledge on a particular social issue or problem, for the purpose of recommending a range of alternatives for resolving it. Policy formulation yields choices among these options, setting general guidelines within which social treatments can be developed. Planning sets priorities among these problem-resolving methods. Program design specifies their content. Program implementation translates a program design into an operating program. Program monitoring oversees the administration, management, and general outcomes of a program for accountability purposes. Scientific evaluation is a systematic study to determine whether a program's effects are consistent with the program's intent and are not due to other factors.

within and between these more rational stages. These influences powerfully oppose any attempt to implement an uninterrupted sequence and limit the potential contributions of policy making and research.

The feedback of research results to policy analysis shows how dynamic the policy cycle can be. The use of research findings is at best tenuous. Research insights and inferences are only one contribution among many compelling ones to the initial study of issues and their formulation, and they may be discounted altogether ultimately. It is true, of course, that they may be more readily valued if they meet the needs of those in control of the policy process, particularly when they legitimize or suppress unacceptable positions. Therefore, although policy researchers must protect their identity as scientists during the conduct of research activities, they will find it necessary to become strong, active advocates for the objective use of their research. This requires participation in the policy process at more than one point, particularly in the earlier stages, to assure that research conclusions have a reasonable chance of influencing decision making.

The income maintenance programs of the 1970s, for example, represented one of our most significant social experiments. At the end of the first wave of data analyses, a national conference was held to disseminate the major findings. Appropriate qualifications were made, and the audience was cautioned that the findings held true only for certain subpopulations of the research sample. Concluding this impressive series of reports, the senior staff counsel for a powerful Senate committee expressed pleasure that these very expensive experiments had confirmed existing political wisdom in Congress that income guarantees encourage people to stop working and their families to break up. This simplistic summary emasculated the data. The next day, however, major national newspapers featured articles reporting the counsel's (not the researchers') conclusions. In short order, the negative income tax concept was relegated mainly to a large number of PhD dissertations and journal articles. A substantial data bank ceased being a source of new policy ideas. The political climate had changed between the concept's inception and testing, and the research had remained largely isolated from the policy process.

It is unfortunate that few policy researchers are consulted by policy analysts or policy makers or present a case for what they can contribute of value through their research. As a result, programs are characteristically evaluated with little or no prior knowledge of their policy chronology. This history is significant because much rhetoric surrounds the social programs to be evaluated. Their public purposes are not necessarily their unwritten political ends. The researcher will need to sort through the polemics and clearly identify what goals and means are most appropriate to study, and on the basis of what assumptions. In this respect, the researcher must search for an understanding of much more than the scientific complexities.

We can only explore a few examples of the many influences within the policy environment that affect research. You may want to immerse yourself in the prolific literature on the policy process in studying this environment more extensively. We shall emphasize only selected political, organizational, and ethical constraints.

### Political Influences
### in the Policy Environment

Political ideologies are keys to the underlying assumptions and premises of social programs. Several general purposes are served by planned change. One is *normative:* social programs arise from a genuine desire to bring the minimum life quality conditions of members of the society into better conformance with the society's democratic, humanitarian, egalitarian values; for example, many programs aim to eliminate poverty and discrimination, alleviate illness and disability, or to provide meaningful work. Another purpose is *political* and *economic*: to change those social conditions the powerful interests in society view as contradictory to their need to maintain control, or that are potentially threatening to their continuance in power. Still another is *organizational*: the need to stabilize economic, political, social, and cultural forces within the society, in the interest of maintaining its internal functioning and its security in the international environment. Political ideologies have a marked effect on the basic goals of social policy initiatives.

These configurations of political beliefs define what social needs, deprivations, injustices (or what possibilities) are to be responded to through the assignment of resources. They affect what groups "deserve" to have their life quality improved or their potential stimulated, and under what circumstances and with what qualifications. They describe what groups do not deserve this response, but instead pose a problem requiring an allocation of resources of a different kind. In both cases they influence the level and content of the response, based on special interest considerations of the costs and benefits.

These rationales therefore shape conceptions of what is a social problem and what is not. They often direct the choices made among a range of possible alternatives for solving problems. The solutions selected frequently become polarized between (1) those intended to ameliorate the effects of uneven life quality or to provide new opportunities for enhancing it, and (2) those that bring the behavior of certain individuals, groups, or social forces under more effective regulation and control. One method of problem-solving is essentially coercive, while the other appeals more to pervasive norms and values. The *kind* of change to which each is committed reveals a continuing tension between two basic forces for social change.

Program designs often incorporate these conflicting mandates, and the researcher must determine which set of changes or what mix of potentially contradictory goals are to be evaluated. The formal legislative intent of most correctional programs for youth is clearly rehabilitative, for example. But are these programs designed to ameliorate the "criminal condition" of the youthful offender through education, job training, or counseling, or are they primarily designed to bring delinquents under tighter control? While usually intending to do both, the setting, services, and even the names of these programs imply a strong emphasis on social control. And it is questionable whether the control aspects of these programs inevitably outweigh their more humanistic purposes.

The researcher must understand the history of American systems of social provision, as these systems have tended to dichotomize social programs in unrealistic ways. Those programs providing services to clients perceived to have earned these services or to deserve them by virtue of prior participation in the life of the society—such as the Social Security program or unemployment insurance—are treated more as rights of citizenship. Those programs responding to clients perceived as having somehow caused their own undesirable condition, who receive services without the appearance of having made a substantial contribution, or who seem to have made a negative one— such as public assistance, Medicaid, or probation and parole services—are treated more as debts owed to society.

Fewer qualifications surround the receipt of services in the first kind of program, and the stigmatizing effect associated with the second kind is considerable. This differentiation between acceptable universalistic guarantees and less acceptable selective responses reveals important assumptions infused throughout the policy process, and most specifically in the planning and design of social innovations and ongoing programs.

Without a sensitivity to the politics of social welfare, and a knowledge of basic program premises, the researcher will not be able to separate the sources of strengths and weaknesses in programs. Policy makers may unwittingly set innovations up to fail if the definition of the basic problem relies too little on objective information and too much on political explanations of reality. Or the social problem may be correctly identified but its causes not appropriately interpreted. Or the program strategy may not fit the problem or address its true causes. The pronouncement of "failure" or "success" may therefore reveal problems at many levels, not simply at the level of a program's conformance to its stated objectives. One of the greatest values of competent policy research is its investigation of the underlying "theories" of planned change and the complex relationships among variables that form and articulate them, as well as the extent to which programs have their intended effect.

### Organizational Influences

Organizations selectively screen and absorb the many influences competing for control over resources in the policy environment. They are the researcher's most immediate environment and affect research activities most directly. The sheer nature of organizations, particularly bureaucracies, has the largest impact on policy research.

All organizations must solve certain basic problems—problems of dividing work, bringing activities together to achieve goals, motivating members to participate through rewards and sanctions, maintaining cohesiveness, and controlling conflict. Resolving these problems stabilizes organizations and clarifies decision-making authority within them. This reduces ambiguity over roles and responsibilities, increases control over goal achievement, and protects personnel from exploitation. It enforces accountability and provides checks on the accumulation of power at the top. Many of the so-called "evils" of bureaucratic development, such as formal hierarchies, formalized processes, rules and regulations, or the specialization of tasks, also assure equity, efficiency, and organizational survival. One failure in implementing social programs may, in fact, be *insufficient* bureaucratization, leading to too little efficiency.[9]

Nevertheless, serious constraints may be imposed on policy research by bureaucratic characteristics such as:

—The tendency to displace the goals of programs, giving higher priority to those goals perceived as critical to maintaining and enhancing an organization's status and position in its environment than to the goals the organization is officially mandated to carry out and for which it is officially held accountable.

—The tendency to engage in power struggles with other organizations perceived as competitors for limited resources, rather than to pool resources to achieve mutual goals through cooperative action.

—The tendency to define innovation and change as inefficient and a threat to the organization's purposes, functions, and security, and therefore to mobilize resources to resist them.

—The tendency to build rigidity into the division of labor and decision-making processes of organizations and for territoriality and competition to develop between and within authority levels.

—The tendency to impose policy decisions from the top without anticipating potential resistances at different decision-making levels or preparing different levels for the possible impact of these changes.

—The tendency to withhold from one level of the organization information needed by another—or to delay, complicate, or distort communication between levels in the interest of maintaining or enhancing the position of personnel at a particular level.

These characteristics direct social programs toward organization-serving goals and mobilize organizational resistance to change. They sometimes close off needed sources of information, support, and cooperation, and cast the researcher in the role of an intruder likely to threaten familiar territories and established views of efficiency and safety.

Perhaps more critical to research, however, is the fact that bureaucracies

---

9. Charles Perrow implies this possibility in his excellent and very interestingly written book, *Complex Organizations* (Glenview, Ill.: Scott, Foresman and Company, 1973).

concentrate an enormous amount of power in a small number of individuals. Although this permits them to organize resources effectively in implementing the broader goals of planned change, it can just as efficiently marshal forces to oppose it. In addition, this power is legitimized through formal, often moralistic organizational "missions" that make it difficult for the researcher to identify the true goals of those in control.

The *actual* "agendas" of these power holders are often more critical to the conduct of research and the control over key variables than all the other organizational features combined. Complicating an understanding of such agendas is the difficulty of detecting the nature of pressures from outside the organization that shape these otherwise more idiosyncratic expectations. If the collective policy scenarios of these significant actors are favorable to the research, some of the other constraints will fall away. If not, they are considerably exacerbated.

### Ethical Issues

It is important to touch briefly on constraints not always given serious attention. The policy researcher faces some very significant dilemmas between competing loyalties to the missions and goals of the funding organization and the organization sustaining the research activities, and the goals of the research itself. Choices or compromises must frequently be made between seizing important career opportunities and participating in research that has the potential for affecting the life quality of certain groups negatively, or that serves the needs of the providers of programs at the expense of those to be benefitted by them. The mandate to implement rigorous research designs sometimes conflicts with the commitment to preserve research subjects' worth, dignity, and civil liberties. Often there are strong pressures on researchers to delay or distort findings or to bias interpretations, and the researcher must decide whether research integrity and credibility are primary.

These issues are difficult to address, but they give policy researchers a unique awareness of the legal, cultural, and moral responsibilities of the research community. Dealing with such issues helps set norms and standards for the professional behavior of research colleagues, and for policy makers and administrators. It encourages the development of formal structures and processes through which the protection of the human subjects of research is better assured.

### IMPLICATIONS FOR THE RESEARCH PROCESS

We have discussed only a few of the many intricacies of the research environment. Even so, we can with confidence assume that influences within the policy setting of research are complex, highly interdependent, resistant to simple study, and that they condition policy research in many subtle and obvious ways. Refocusing our attention on the research process, we want to propose some implications this inscrutable policy environment has on research tasks, using conceptualization, measurement, and research design as examples.

## Conceptualization and Measurement

Policy research is often stereotyped as "atheoretical" because it lacks both explanatory models constructed from empirical findings and those drawn from a body of established theoretical propositions and hypotheses. This judgment has its source in the pragmatic, often nonintellectual *purposes* and *contexts* of policy research. But the problem is not a paucity of knowledge about potential variables, relationships, or underlying assumptions. Rather, it lies in the researcher's ability to identify and retrieve theoretical propositions from the policy process through which planned change is generated. What most distinguishes policy research is the difficulty the researcher has in developing an adequate, comprehensive explanatory model unhampered by organizational and social-political constraints, and the absence of a clearly specified set of relationships in the research proposal appropriate to the complexity of the program or the problem it addresses.

Also, social programs introduce change artificially. The environment receiving the impact of this kind of change has not been created primarily for research purposes. It is an environment that receives many other kinds of changes consciously introduced by other constituencies. It receives the effects of many regularly occurring unprogrammed influences. One particular set of treatments, the program to be evaluated, must therefore be distinguishable by the researcher from the myriad of other treatments operating simultaneously. The ability of these other treatments to produce changes in the research subjects must be separated from the singular effects of the program. Therefore the development of a theoretical explanation that will support an adequate research design for differentiating among these influences is the first and often the most difficult task in policy research.

To illustrate a few of these difficulties, suppose the researcher is evaluating a residential program providing services to women who have temporarily left relationships involving physical or emotional abuse. The federal statute and regulations authorizing this program state simply that these women are to be provided temporary housing, other basic essentials, and services intended to increase their economic and psychological independence. The latter are the independent variables inherited by the researcher for use in a theoretical model.

The researcher is aware that a knowledge of the combination of forces that brought the issue of "battered women" to the attention of Congress and shaped this particular solution will provide assumptions important to the construction of a model, as it suggests important additional variables to incorporate. It is clear to the researcher also that the most significant independent variable may be the type of facility providing the services, rather than the services themselves, and that there are numerous influences operating to change these women's behavior and attitudes other than the facility *or* the services.

However, none of these additional theoretical considerations have been specified in the research contract. Nor has the particular condition to be changed been clearly specified, or the type or degree of the expected change been made sufficiently explicit to easily identify the dependent variable. Are these women to leave abusive relationships permanently, or are they to behave in ways that will reduce abuse within these relationships? And for how long and under what conditions?

Very often the researcher has received only a very vague picture of the set of relationships to be studied and must be unusually creative in constructing them. Let us briefly explore some of the dimensions of these and related conceptual and measurement problems.

*Premises and Assumptions.* The initial statement of relationships is often a very simple causal one. The funder proposes that the program treatments are responsible for the desired changes in the consumers of the program's services. This general causal statement must then be recast by the researcher into measurable variables and into a set of relationships among variables. It is at this point in the conceptualization process that the most generous opportunities are available for adding important variables to a theoretical framework that will guide the evaluation of a program. It is in sorting out the premises that the researcher has the least *intellectual* constraints and can reap significant benefits.

*The Program Treatments.* The "planned" independent variable is ordinarily not as *unitary* as it appears. Several sets of independent variables are subsumed under "the program," such as those describing the way the program is influenced by its internal organizational environment, the manner in which the agency administers the program, the kind of service delivery system providing the program treatments, as well as the components of the actual services and monetary benefits to be received by the program's clients. The content of the program and its environmental influences involve many more variables than the simple statement of goals and means bequeathed to the researcher initially. Furthermore, the characteristics of these independent variables do not remain fixed. They tend to vary in the process of implementation and evaluation, as a function of: the length of a program's history; the extent to which administrative, management, or service delivery changes have occurred; changes taking place in the consumers; and influences external to the program and its setting. The theoretical model must reflect these complexities.

"Unplanned" independent variables that affect program outcomes have multiple aspects also. These represent rival explanations that must be anticipated in the theoretical model. For many programs, broad economic or demographic changes affecting the clients or programs may be critical; so also will be the effects of other social programs providing similar services, the influences of relatives and friends who provide spontaneous social services meeting the same needs, or the simple act of being studied.

*The Condition to Be Changed.*    The dependent variable that is "given" usually represents a *cluster* of variables ranging from those descriptive of some arbitrary threshold defined as an "undesirable" condition, to those descriptive of some optimal "desirable" one. The actual endpoints of the continuum are not well specified for the researcher, and better definition and measurement must be anticipated in the theoretical model. Points on the continuum must be resolved, such as the degree of difference between an abstract undesirable condition (for instance, "psychological and economic dependence") and a desirable condition (such as "psychological and economic self-sufficiency"). In clarifying the independent and dependent variables that describe social progams more fully, the researcher has far more license to develop sufficient theoretical frameworks than one would at first suppose.

*Relationships Between Variables.*    The statement of relationships between independent and dependent variables often conveys how these variables *ought* to be related, not how they may actually *be* related. While all propositions and hypotheses state probabilities that relationships will be of a particular kind, these probabilities are normally based on prior scientific knowledge and insights. In policy research, the linkages are more representative of the subjective judgments of powerful groups. The refinement of these simpler, subjective statements of relationships into more specific objective statements of association, and sometimes cause-and-effect, can be very complex. Subsequent research activities, however, will be conditioned by the level of sophisticaton of these restatements, the quality of the theoretical properties brought together, and the researcher's general knowledge and inventiveness in deciding which variables are to be related to what others, in what way, under what circumstances, using what research subjects, and why.

Unfortunately, the hypotheses received from others may sometimes involve *too many* treatments and outcomes. The researcher must select those variables most useful to test, and choose among potential propositions interrelating them. Planners and designers sometimes assume all variables in a complicated program are equally measurable and manipulable when they are not. The explanatory model should not be allowed to overwhelm the rest of the research process. The researcher should build into the model a guide to the expected *progression of changes* leading to the desired ones, indicating the points in this chronology where certain relationships may be most critical to measure. This alerts the investigator to modifications that may need to be made in the model, and possibly in the measures.

*Those to Whom the Model Applies.*    Some research propositions state linkages between treatments and resulting conditions that apply only to particular clients of programs, usually not selected by the researcher. As we pointed out earlier, these research subjects are not usually representative of the larger population of potential recipients of other kinds of planned change, or of the general public. By definition, they exhibit "problematic" conditions that require a "programmatic" response. For example, families with incomes below the federal income threshold are considered "economically disadvantaged," whether they perceive themselves to be so or not. Programs are therefore designed to resolve this economic problem in ways these potential consumers may or may not prefer. Fortunately, most consumers have a choice in receiving the service, but it is certainly not the same kind of choice they have in purchasing products in other systems of exchange. Theoretical models must therefore carefully detail to whom the explanatory model is applicable, and state qualifications to the model if the results are intended to be more widely generalized.

*Sources of Conceptual Bias.*    These difficulties are complicated by the pervasive influence in policy research of classic economic theories and measures. Economic frameworks are often characterized by a limited set of variables, narrow quantitative measures, and extensive (and sometimes unwarranted) assumptions about what variables can be ignored in the explanation of relationships. The application of such economic models and profit-oriented market assumptions to the study of social problems and programs is often inappropriate.[10] Many important sociological, psychological, and other social science variables are frequently neglected.

Business and accounting approaches are a related source of bias. These orientations are expressed in the design of computerized information systems, through which data on programs are collected and tabulated for accountability purposes. These complex, expensive, and sometimes unreliable information systems have been developed to administer and oversee programs, not to evaluate them. Since these systems primarily serve the credibility needs of program funders, their variables and measures reflect business and economic definitions of efficiency. It is often impossible for the researcher to retrieve a full range of data on individual characteristics and program history, data which are necessary to an analysis of the relationship between treatments and effect. Yet the researcher is often expected to rely on these systems as a major source of data.

In this sense, the way in which accountability is viewed tends to control the program's ultimate form, irrespective of its original goals. Researchers must be adept in retaining their professional identity, and preserving their independence from such biases.

---

10. Economic orientations impose significant constraints even in well-conceived field experiments that emphasize a longitudinal research approach. The explanatory models have often proposed too-simple causal relationships between a small number of variables and used too few measures, all narrowly oriented toward standard economic factors and indices. Even though such experiments may be *carefully* implemented, their findings may be of limited value for this reason.

## Research Design

Design issues are a central concern in policy research. Although design tasks are complicated by the same environmental constraints as other parts of the research process, the researcher is free to use a growing inventory of scientific techniques in developing research designs. The major difficulty, however, is interference with the use of experimental procedures. In resolving difficulties that mar the validity or generalizability of research findings, policy researchers have often had to turn to designs that required substantial compromises with experimental principles.[11]

Prior randomization of the recipients of treatments is a key design tool, and the most difficult to incorporate in policy research. But it provides the necessary assurance that *random* processes, rather than biases, will determine the selection of the experimental group receiving the program's services, and the control or comparison groups not receiving them. Differences found to exist between these groups can then be more boldly attributed to the interventions consciously introduced than to other influences. But random assignment is not only difficult, it is sometimes inequitable and dehumanizing in many policy research contexts.

In evaluating the benefits of in-home skilled nursing care for elderly patients as an alternative to nursing home care, how would the researcher justify a random assignment of a pool of elderly patients to their own homes or to nursing homes? In studying community alternatives to commitment of mentally ill individuals in mental hospitals, how would the researcher justify a random assignment of psychotic patients to mental institutions or to community residential care facilities? New social program strategies are often considered an "enrichment." Whether they are or not, novel approaches are thus seen as inequitable in the eyes of clients receiving traditional services. The perception of inequality, in itself, may affect the outcomes of such innovations. And there is the possibility that the experimental group will be substantially affected simply by being selected for study.

But clearly it is preferable to conform to experimental design principles. As mentioned in Chapter 4, research designs that approximate these principles are often called *quasi-experimental*. Their purpose is to compensate for the absence of randomization and for weakened control over key variables. They guide the researcher in resolving certain kinds of challenges to *validity* and *generalizability* that are more prevalent in the policy environment than elsewhere. Tables 6–1 and 6–2 summarize and illustrate some of these basic problems.

---

11. One of the best sources and the most basic work on validity and generalizability is Donald T. Campbell and Julian C. Stanley's excellent short book, *Experimental and Quasi-Experimental Designs for Research* (Chicago: Rand McNally College Publishing Company, 1963).

| CHALLENGES TO VALIDITY | EXAMPLE | PROBLEM POSED |
|---|---|---|
| 1. Influences *other than* the experimental variable (the program treatments) that operate between the first measurement (of the "before" condition of the research subjects) and the second measurement (of their "after" condition). | Events occurring between these measurements such as:<br>—political events affecting the way the administering agency implements the program<br>—economic events that intervene to change perceptions of desired outcomes.<br>—attitudinal changes on the part of staff or research subjects produced by favorable or unfavorable media coverage of the program. | These events or attitudinal changes may be the key independent variables rather than the program. |
| 2. Changes in the characteristics of the research subjects due to *naturally occurring processes* independent of the program that are related to the length of the time period during which the research subjects are measured. | Biological and psychological processes in individuals, and developmental processes in organizations. Examples include becoming older, more knowledgeable, or developing new physical features, or becoming more bureaucratized, less flexible, or more vulnerable to public pressure. | Normal individual growth patterns, family life cycles, or organizational evolution may be the best explanation for the differences found, rather than the treatment. |
| 3. Effects on research subjects due to the sheer *influence of measures being collected* on their characteristics, particularly the influence of the first measurement on subsequent measurements. | Increased awareness of what information may be most acceptable, increased trust in the confidentiality of the data-gathering effort, different attitudes toward the data gatherer. | Being sensitized to the status of "research subject" may be causing the effects observed, not the program. |
| 4. Changes in the *way* measures are collected or in the *characteristics* of the collectors. | Rearrangements in interview formats, or rewording of questionnaire items: new approaches used by interviewers or different packaging | Manipulations of the measuring instruments may bias the results, independent of the treatments. |

*(cont.)*

Table 6-1 Challenges to Validity (cont.)

| CHALLENGES TO VALIDITY | EXAMPLE | PROBLEM POSED |
|---|---|---|
| | of questionnaires; burn-out on the part of the research subject or the data gatherer. | |
| 5. Measurement errors related to before/after measurements on social program client populations, due to *the nature of these target groups*—i.e., their tendency to represent the "extreme" ends of continua that describe regular populations. | In studying a program providing counseling to emotionally disturbed children, the researcher will be selecting children whose mental health status is at one extreme of the continuum on this variable. Selection processes are never perfect and always produce some errors. In this case, there will be certain children measured before the treatments are introduced who are considered to be ill but they are actually closer to the average. A second measurement may reflect a truer estimation of their status. This would give the impression that the program was responsible for a great improvement, when faulty initial measurement was responsible. | Analyzing differences between groups selected as "extremes" may result in attributing effects to treatments that are actually due to measurement error. |
| 6. Biases due to the differential way in which the target group and comparison groups are *selected*. | Students identified through *special testing* as having a particular cluster of learning problems, and a group identified by their parents as having such problems, are likely not to represent sufficiently similar problems | The measures on the treated vs. comparison groups may represent different variables. If students identified by their parents have more severe problems, for example, than those screened through testing, the |

Table   6-1      Challenges to Validity (*cont.*)

| CHALLENGES TO VALIDITY | EXAMPLE | PROBLEM POSED |
|---|---|---|
| | (or problems of the same magnitude) to be considered approximately "equivalent" for comparison purposes.<br><br>The treated group of students may be found to differ substantially from the untreated group, but the differences in outcomes may simply reflect differences in the characteristics of the selection process. | "treated" group may appear to have made less progress than is actually the case. |
| 7. Effects of *losing* members from treatment and comparison groups nonrandomly, therefore losing after measures nonrandomly. | In a study of displaced homemakers, for example, there may be a treated group receiving career counseling and job assistance, and a comparison group who do not receive these services. A differential loss of women from these groups could introduce biases into the final assessment of the outcomes of the program. Since after measurements would be unavailable on those lost, the findings would reflect changes occurring only for those left in these two groups. If those left in the treatment group differed (in ways related to the variables being studied) from those left in the comparison group, the extent of change due to career counseling and job services may reflect this phenomenon as much as it does the effect of the program. | Differential losses in treated and nontreated groups may introduce biases into the findings that are difficult to identify and correct. |

**Table 6-2    Challenges to Generalizability**

| CHALLENGES TO GENERALIZABILITY | EXAMPLE | PROBLEM POSED |
|---|---|---|
| 1. Effects due to *participation* in a research project that result in reactions by research subjects not necessarily typical of the larger group from which they are drawn. | Increased responsiveness of the research subjects in a time-limited negative income tax study to the temporary attractiveness of decreased work effort, as compared with the longer-term reactions of low-income individuals in the general population receiving benefits from a negative income tax over a more normal period of time. | Treatment effects observed in a short-term or pilot project may not hold true when applied over longer periods in accustomed settings under more normal conditions. (For example, work effort may not decrease under the latter conditions.) |
| 2. Effects due to the *interaction* between biases introduced in the selection of treatment and comparison groups, and the treatments themselves. | If women felons with characteristics favorable to the productive use of residential alternatives to prison are selected to receive residential programs, the observed program effects will be great simply due to the interaction between these characteristics (such as motivation to conform to residential rules) and rules or regulations provided as one of the treatments. | The program is destined by definition to produce the desired outcomes, not because of the treatments per se, but because of the prior motivation, attitudes, or other characteristics of the women selected, which are automatically enhanced by the treatments. In the absence of self-selection, the results might be quite different, making the program difficult to generalize to larger populations. |
| 3. Effects due to the attempt to *approximate experimental conditions,* leading to findings that may not hold true for less-experimental settings and conditions. | Subjects isolated for the purposes of controlled measurement may think and behave differently from the way they would under normal conditions. | Rival explanations for the research findings may be significantly different for a cloistered vs. real-life setting in which treatments would be introduced in a larger population. |
| 4. Effects due to the *interaction* between multiple treatments applied to the same recipients. | A program for structurally unemployed workers may rationally provide services in a particular sequence, such as basic education, followed by skill training, followed by job placement. The ef- | The residues of the effects of prior treatments remain to influence the response to subsequent treatments, making it difficult to generalize collective program outcomes to other populations. |

Table 6-2    Challenges to Generalizability (cont.)

| CHALLENGES TO GENERALIZABILITY | EXAMPLE | PROBLEM POSED |
|---|---|---|
| | fects of each of the three may interact with one another such that the separate effects are difficult to determine. If these were provided in other combinations or sequences to larger populations, the combined outcomes might be different. | |

We will mention only a few quasi-experimental approaches, but we encourage you to investigate the excellent literature on this subject.[12] For example, if a program is fairly well established, or if all the treatments are to be delivered to each client, the researcher can sort out the effects of "non-program" treatments or additional explanations by taking "before" and "after" measures on a group comparable to the group receiving the program. For instance, if the researcher is studying the effects of a drug education program on a group of suburban adolescents, another group of adolescents could be selected who had comparable key characteristics but were not receiving the drug program. Results from these groups could then be compared. In this case, self-selection into the comparison group, and differences in the two research environments, would need to be anticipated and avoided.

This kind of conscious, knowledgeable selection of a comparison group can involve either a careful *matching of individuals* or a matching of the *distribution of general group characteristics*. The choice of methods and the closeness of the match are dependent on the potential number of appropriate individuals to choose from, the accuracy of the criteria used, and the time and monetary resources available to accomplish the task. It usually is less problematic, if the comparison groups are selected on the basis of similar *collective* characteristics, a procedure that requires considerable statistical expertise.

Another design strategy is to use program recipients *themselves* as controls over additional explanatory variables. This depends on making a series of measurements of program participants at different predictable time intervals prior to the implementation of the program and over its history. Clients entering the service delivery system at different points in that history ideally

12.  Clear, nontechnical, and very competent discussions of design issues can be found in Peter Rossi, Howard Freeman, and Sonia Wright's *Evaluation: A Systematic Approach* referred to earlier; Carol A. Weiss's *Evaluation Research* (Englewood Cliffs, N. J.: Prentice-Hall, Inc., 1972); Howard Freeman and Clarence Sherwood's *Social Research and Social Policy* (Englewood Cliffs, N. J.: Prentice-Hall, Inc., 1970). Our discussion of designs draws substantially from the ideas presented in these books.

would be measured prior to receiving the program, at periodic regular intervals during the course of their participation in the program, at the end of their participation, and for a period following termination in the program.

An extensive knowledge of the condition or status of the program's consumers prior to receiving the program is necessary to treating these "before" measures *as if* they represented measures on a comparison group. The adequacy of this knowledge depends on the number of measures collected on these individuals or entities, and the length of the time period during which they were gathered before the program began or before the client entered the program. The longer the time period and the more frequent the measurements, the more accurate the researcher can be in developing criteria for judging desired outcomes against the actual ones.

Some designs attempt to compensate for the absence of even a quasi-experimental group. These strategies involve developing *estimates* of treatment effects. The data used may not be representative of individuals with extensive similarities to the treated individuals, except with respect to a few characteristics considered representative of other common characteristics. Comparability is achieved through statistical analyses applied to measures collected at a single point in time.

For example, in studying the treatment effects of an alternative to incarceration, the researcher might compare *ex-felons* receiving the alternative program with those with similar characteristics who had been in prison during the same period and in the same community setting. However, these two groups may differ because of the way they were selected by the researcher, or because of differential (and unmeasured) influences in the prison and non-prison environments. Even relying entirely on these statistical estimates of effects, prior measurements as well as after measurements would increase the level of control. If the researcher had both sets of recidivism rates for the period immediately after release and also at a later date, the accuracy and magnitude of treatment effects would be better understood. All of these approaches should incorporate ways to compare measures for those treated with those not treated. This vastly increases the researcher's faith in the ultimate findings, assuming the measurement process itself does not affect the outcomes.[13]

We do not want to imply that to be considered competent and useful, policy research should obsessively pursue experimental principles. The stress on experimental models has often been faulted for holding the definition of program variables constant at the expense of allowing ongoing improvements

---

13.   The use of statistical estimates as controls is too complex to discuss here, but they are useful in both experimental and quasi-experimental designs. They are most useful if the researcher's purpose is to separate out the effects of different interventions on subsets of the target group, or to sort out interactive effects.

in the program design to be made, and for the way in which causal anlaysis objectives are pursued.[14] Some policy researchers feel that an overemphasis on experimentation has too narrowly dominated recent developments in program evaluation. Researchers have been led to regard programs as fixed and unchanging, to force programs to fit quasi-experimental designs, to use control groups that do not control important variables, or to select comparison groups that are not comparable. Even prior randomization procedures are sometimes accused of changing the nature of realistic program processes. Some of these criticisms are unfounded; however, conformity to experimental design features has sometimes been rigidly overdefined and has taken too little advantage of the flexibility that exists. Experimentation has sometimes proved unreplicable, and its theoretical underpinnings shaky. Its deserved prestige should not result in a discrediting of nonexperimental wisdom that has often been extremely insightful and useful. Certain programs and environments may lend themselves to experimental designs in policy research, while others clearly require approximate or clearly nonexperimental approaches.

In general, nonexperimental designs allow the researcher to take a *preliminary* look at both program implementation and impact. A beginning assessment can be made of whether the changes observed look substantial, or provide other clues to the value of further study. Also, since some policy researchers are confined by their contracts to one-time "after" evaluations, well-conceived nonexperimental designs may stimulate funders to initiate more systematic research.

## SOME CONTRIBUTIONS
## OF POLICY RESEARCH

We have emphasized the difficulties involved in policy research. Despite sizeable constraints, however, it has made valuable contributions to other social researchers and the social science knowledge base; to policy makers and program designers; and to the resolution of life quality issues. It has sensitized social scientists to significant variables often taken for granted or consciously neglected. It has afforded pragmatic tests for evaluating traditional theoretical models and methods, thus stimulating insights, research design innovations, and new propositions and hypotheses for more systematic study. The organizational skills acquired by policy researchers have fostered a more supportive political environment for research activity and increased the integra-

---

14. An informative discussion of this perspective is Marcia Guttentag, Ward Edwards, and Kurt Snapper's provocative article, "Decision-Theoretic Approach to Evaluation Research" in the *Handbook of Evaluation Research*, Vol. 1, edited by Edward L. Struening and Marcia Guttentag (London: Sage Publications, 1975).

tion of research findings across diverse disciplines. Although less tangible, policy research has increased decision makers' and program administrators' understanding of the complexity and intractability of social problems, placing expectations for problem resolution in more realistic perspective and reinforcing greater rationality in the use of funds for social purposes.

These benefits continue to be realized unevenly, and there are strong pressures to use policy research simply to legitimate the appropriateness of previous decisions, to satisfy powerful unwritten political and organizational goals, and to postpone decision making in order to avoid controversy, opposition, or loss of control over resources. The policy researcher must of necessity become a research lobbyist and serious student of utilization issues, the subject of the final chapter.

# CHAPTER 7
# THE UTILIZATION
# OF RESEARCH

Intelligence is quickness to apprehend, as distinct from ability, which is capacity to act wisely on the thing apprehended.

So much has been written in the last decade about the expansion of knowledge and its use that we often forget that bridging the chasm between generating ideas and facts and assuring their appropriate use is an ancient, persistent problem. The meaning of this concept has itself been an historical enigma. What *kind* of use is implied? Short term or over an extended period of social history? Usefulness for what *purpose*? The growth of science? The art of policy making? The improvement of societies? The accumulation of wealth and power?

And for *whom* is it to be useful? Those who control major human and physical resources? The humanitarians among us? The opportunists? Are there universal values that form the criteria for identifying improved bodies of knowledge, better-functioning societies, more effective solutions to social problems, or political exploitation? Even the simple, well-known remark that "knowledge is power" has its subtle complexities. Clearly the misuse, abuse, or suppression of knowledge may constitute power. And those in power may choose to ignore the knowledge that is available to them.

Raising utilization issues such as these should be an integral part of the researcher's initial training and ongoing professional socialization, though this aspect of academic apprenticeship is often neglected. This neglect has risks with respect to the direction research may take. The significant decisions made about what kinds of research will be funded, who will be selected to perform it, and how it will be used, already favor the priorities of nonresearchers.

A disturbing example of the need for researchers to become more alert to utilization issues is the severe curtailment of federal support for the social, behavioral, and economic sciences in 1981. Without consulting the scientific community, or even the National Science Board, the Office of Management and Budget substantially reduced the National Science Foundation's budget for social science research, at the same time preserving funding for the applied physical sciences. This decision was reportedly premised on an ideological distaste for those areas of science in which the findings were less quantitative and less easily converted to fiscal measures. It was based also on the perception that these research areas had provided data relevant to social initiatives and programs now at variance with new economic priorities.

For the first time in several decades, a judgment had been made about the social legitimacy of particular fields of scientific inquiry without the benefit of competent scientific advice. However, this significant change in federal support for the social sciences reflected an ignorance of the substantial benefits associated with studying problems not easily amenable to objective measurement, particularly in a period in which the society faced unusually complex domestic and international problems demanding a much greater understanding of social and economic behavior. This unprecedented action, however, served to politicize the social research community, to sensitize researchers to the need for collective action around issues of research preference, support and utilization, and to encourage a re-evaluation of the growing dependence of scientific research on federal needs and priorities.

Social researchers cannot afford to compromise their objectivity or their identity as scientists in the process of carrying out research activities. However, they no longer have the luxury of remaining aloof from utilization problems and possibilities. They have an increasingly serious obligation to defend the benefits of their work. Also, if researchers are not concerned about the potential negative effects of their investigations on the well-being of individuals and groups or the impact on social institutions, or if research findings are permitted to be misinterpreted or made to serve questionable purposes without protest, then the value of participation in research is open to debate.

Encouraging more appropriate research, reducing the overdependence of social researchers on only a few sources of funding, and actively supporting the proper use of research requires strong convictions and important skills complementary to research expertise. While the researcher's persuasiveness may be limited in its effect, efforts to convey the outcomes of research truthfully, and to assure its use at opportune points in decision making processes, can have an important impact. The general trend toward greater reliance on a scientific basis for planning, budgeting and forecasting in the allocation of major resources supports this advocacy.

## UTILIZATION PROBLEMS

There are a number of utilization issues we need to be aware of.[1] The most basic is the scientific adequacy of the research. Unfortunately the quality of the research process does not always guarantee that the findings will be appropriately used. Yet the issue of training and competence should be an important concern of the research consumer. Given research of high quality, its relevance to previous theory and research or to accumulated policy experience is another important issue. Again, this kind of relevance is often less compelling in determining its use than the immediate social, political or organizational significance of the research topic.

The fact that the federal government has for some time been the primary benefactor of social research has utilization implications. Government funding has favored specific policy-relevant research questions over the production of general knowledge with broader application. Furthermore, government decisions have been deeply enmeshed in bureaucratic, legislative, and special interest politics. Increasing external pressures on governmental research divisions to demonstrate the value of research to policy formulators, program managers, and legislators concerned with immediate social crises or problems has limited perspectives on what is feasible and desirable to promote, disseminate, and utilize. There are basic conflicts and tensions between policy and research processes themselves. Rapidly changing events and influences direct the policy process informally toward prompt, inexpensive, quantitative proof, social utility, and political feasibility. The research process, by contrast, is conditioned formally by standardized procedures that guide its focus toward research quality and away from subjectivity, a stance that resists short-term cost-effective approaches. Also, there are too few economic and ideological incentives for the following:

—the general coordination of research activities,

—research that cuts across diverse issues and settings,

—comparative and long-term studies,

—the integration of existing findings and the closing of gaps in knowledge,

—the identification of potential research users,

—the development of policies and procedures for encouraging dissemination and utilization,

---

1. The discussion of utilization problems and possibilities uses some of the excellent ideas and recommendations in the first comprehensive study of federal support for social knowledge production and application. See *The Federal Investment in Knowledge of Social Problems,* final report of the Study Project of the Office of Science and Technology Policy (Washington, D.C.: National Science Foundation, 1974).

—a better understanding of change and innovation, and

—the clarification of governmental versus nongovernmental roles in the communication and use of findings.

Several other utilization issues deserve attention. The researcher, funder, or decision maker may overgeneralize research findings for immediate use, rather than allow data on a series of related studies to accumulate prior to dissemination and application. And there has been only minimal validation of findings through replication or secondary analyses of existing bodies of data. The results of research are often not communicated to decision makers or planners at the most advantageous times in terms of their own time frames or moments of peak relevance in the political process, or in a desirable, usable form (succinct, brief, and without complex qualifications). Potential research users seeking information on research questions relevant to them are not well organized to pursue systematic searches, or adequately rewarded for attempting to do so. In addition, the professionalization of policy research, and its misidentification as a distinct field of research with its own technology, has made it difficult to bring policy and nonpolicy research findings together usefully.

Also there are deficiencies in the initial selection of research issues and the definition of research questions that reduce the ultimate utility of research. Congress, for example, is given responsibility for setting research priorities and defining their measurable objectives, when it should more appropriately be developing general policies and goals. Federal agencies further restrict the usefulness of research in responding to Congressional mandates through administrative rules and regulations. Both practices lead to:

—unclear or too limited formulations of research agendas,

—research questions for which the required evidence is not likely to be gathered reliably,

—unrealistic expectations for the use of findings,

—biases in the direction of justifying or rejecting existing policy, rather than altering policy, or suggesting policy innovations,

—selection of the wrong research problem or oversimplification of the problem, and

—an emphasis on effects rather than causes, such as the social and institutional structures within which a specific social problem arises.

Beyond these issues, research is too often deliberately misused. It is sometimes used for the following unanticipated purposes:

—to legitimate previous policies,

—to satisfy organizational accountability requirements,

—to selectively support prior positions,

—to cancel an entire program or negate a major idea,

—to suppress results that are not flattering to established legislative or administrative interests,

—to postpone needed but controversial action,

—to compromise accurate results because of fiscal and time pressures,

—to prejudice the dissemination of results due to nonresearch interpretations,

—to receive results in a biased manner because of the consumer's needs, and

—to delay a decision in order to allow an issue to die.

## NEW POSSIBILITIES

An appreciation of the realities in communicating and using research can readily translate to unnecessary cynicism. Although researchers cannot resolve the dilemmas that accompany the use of their work, they can choose to clarify these conflicts in more effective ways and to make more explicit the probable consequences of decisions made by others.

One of the more important contributions researchers can make is to insist on better integration of the ways in which most research is funded, monitored, communicated, and applied. Significant new opportunities would be possible if the administration and regulation of research activities were transferred to formal, politically neutral oversight bodies. If such bodies were to rely more heavily on analysts and decision makers with a technical knowledge of research and the needs of major consumers, they could standardize the processes for funding, planning, assessing, communicating, and using research, based on criteria that reflect scientific more than political or organizational judgments.

The intent of such bodies would be to support multi-year funding, replication, comparative studies, research that cross-cuts diverse issues, and the accumulation of theoretical and empirical knowledge prior to carrying out full-scale studies of complex problems. The purpose would also be to encourage a more intense and persistent dialogue between policy makers and researchers, coordinate research planning and monitoring with policy and program development and assessment, and provide stronger incentives to institutions and organizations that play an integrative decision-making or planning role with respect to a range of research issues and projects.

Such a new era of accountability would provide an immediate opportunity to redefine the value of social knowledge and its utilization, and to reveal the negative, wasteful consequences of developing policy and pursuing knowledge in its absence. It would give more attention to the complex social problems that are the source of the narrower circumscribed problems to which so much research has been directed. It would encourage research on the process and implications of social change.

Pragmatically, a restructuring of research administration and supervision could lead to a more sensitive, knowledgeable incorporation of the needs of research consumers and subjects into the planning, dissemination, and utilization of research. It would likely increase the quality of research and the selectivity with which findings are released and used. It would allow the researcher to be a policy consultant, diplomat, negotiator, and information exchange agent, as the situation warranted. The policy process could thus include knowledge brokers committed to channeling research information to policymakers at the right times and in the most desirable formats. Out of such a period might come new perspectives and strategies for sythesizing inferences from the existing rich, pluralistic research spectrum, and a stronger consensus about the circumstances under which it should be used.

Researchers have an important part to play in creating these new *possibilities*. However, they will need to put aside partisan research territoriality and organize around a common interest in studying social phenomena, if scientists and decision makers are to deal with these phenomena at an appropriate level of complexity. Divisiveness among those oriented more to theory than to methodology, to quantitative rather than to qualitative data, and to social problems more than to underlying social structures, will need to be relegated to intrafamilial debates. Social scientists will need to present a unified position in behalf of the advancement of knowledge and life quality. Researchers who evaluate policy initiatives must become as interested in why social programs are justified as they are in what makes them work. Researchers who study less policy-useful problems must give equal attention to basic issues generated by social change and the conditions of social life.

These plausible new directions can, of course, have negative as well as positive outcomes. They can, for instance, increase the politicization and regulation of research. Or they can capitalize on the growing legislative and managerial sophistication about the technical aspects of research, and the rising expectations for its quality and usefulness. In either case, there must be greater activity to assure rationality in producing and integrating knowledge. While the ultimate form of communication and use will be designed largely by others, researchers can set influential norms, values, and precedents that subtly fashion that final image.

# SOME SUGGESTED READINGS

## General Texts

BABBIE, EARL R. *The Practice of Social Research,* 2nd ed. Belmont, Calif.: Wadsworth Publishing Co., 1973.

BLALOCK, HUBERT M. *Theory Construction.* Englewood Cliffs, N. J.: Prentice-Hall, Inc., 1969.

CAMPBELL, DONALD T., and JULIAN C. STANLEY. *Experimental and Quasi-Experimental Designs for Research.* Chicago: Rand McNally College Publishing Company, 1963.

ECKHARDT, KENNETH W., and M. DAVID ERMANN. *Social Research Methods.* New York: Random House, 1977.

MANHEIM, HENRY L. *Sociological Research: Philosophy and Methods.* Homewood, Ill.: Dorsey Press, 1977.

SANDERS, WILLIAM B. *The Sociologist as Detective,* 2nd ed. New York: Praeger Publishers, 1976.

SELLTIZ, CLAIRE, LAWRENCE S. WRIGHTSMAN, and STUART COOK. *Research Methods in Social Relations,* 3rd ed. New York: Holt, Rinehart & Winston, 1976.

SMITH, H. W. *Strategies of Social Research.* Englewood Cliffs, N. J.: Prentice-Hall, Inc., 1981.

## Books on Policy Research

FREEMAN, HOWARD E., and CLARENCE C. SHERWOOD. *Social Research and Social Policy.* Englewood Cliffs, N. J.: Prentice-Hall, Inc., 1970.

ROSSI, PETER H., HOWARD E. FREEMAN, and SONIA R. WRIGHT. *Evaluation: A Systematic Approach.* London: Sage Publications, 1979.

SUCHMAN, EDWARD A. *Evaluative Research*. New York: Russell Sage Foundation, 1967.

WEISS, CAROL H. *Evaluation Research*. Englewood Cliffs, N. J.: Prentice-Hall, Inc., 1972.

# INDEX